The Inaugural Story

INAUGURATION OF ★ ★ PRESIDENT AND VICE PRESIDENT

NIXON AGNEW

The Inaugural Story
1789~1969

Created and Produced by
The Editors of AMERICAN HERITAGE MAGAZINE
and THE 1969 INAUGURAL BOOK COMMITTEE

The first inauguration as depicted on a bronze door at the Capitol in Washington.

$\mathscr{C}$ontents

Introduction

The inauguration of a President is the high point in the four-year cycle of the American government. It is a solemn occasion; it is a gala occasion; it is a time of pomp and circumstance and of the pageantry and gaiety of parades, balls, and receptions.

Yet none of this celebration and only one small bit of the ceremony is necessary to install a President. The Constitution has only one simple requirement of the President-elect: it prescribes the simple oath that he must take, in which he promises to execute faithfully the office of President and to defend the Constitution. That is all there is to it. All else that happens on an Inauguration Day is custom and tradition, accumulated over the almost two centuries since George Washington became the first President.

When Richard Milhous Nixon became the 37th President of the United States, he stood in the shadow of 180 years of history. He repeated, word for word, the same oath that George Washington had taken in 1789; he delivered his Inaugural Address from the portico of the Capitol as James Polk and Abraham Lincoln and William McKinley had done before him; and after the ceremony he rode down Pennsylvania Avenue as had Andrew Jackson, Ulysses Grant, Woodrow Wilson, and both the Roosevelts.

It is a good and comforting thing that so much of the past looks over the shoulder of the present when a President is inaugurated. It reassures every American citizen, even those apprehensive of change, that the nation is in good hands; that policies may change, but the Presidency remains unaltered. The inauguration of President Nixon has already taken its place in history, and something of what happened on January 20, 1969, will almost certainly be woven into future inaugural ceremonies and celebrations, to become part of the fabric of tradition.

Because so much of the venerable past is present at an inauguration, it is difficult to tell the story of today without often looking backward to see when and how a custom arose. For that reason, the Inaugural Book and Program Committee elected to tell the story of the events of Inauguration Day, 1969, against the backdrop of inauguration days long faded into dim memory. Toward that end was created *The Inaugural Story*.

J. (for John) Willard Marriott, right, was the architect of the 1969 inaugural. Born in 1900, the son of a Mormon rancher in Utah, he came to Washington after college and, starting with a root-beer stand, built a corporation that now owns—among other interests—a chain of restaurants, motels, and catering services. Shown with him above is his wife, the former Alice Sheets, whom he married in 1927. She is a vice chairman of the Inaugural Committee.

A Message from the Chairman

An inauguration is many things. It is, of course, the time when the American political process comes to full fruition. It is the tangible conclusion of months of intensive political campaigning. It is, in the person of the new President, the embodiment of the right of free choice—the investiture of an elected Chief of State, chosen by more than seventy million of his countrymen.

Naturally, the inauguration is a time of great symbolism and pageantry; a time of joy as well as solemnity. In inaugurating the 37th President of the United States, we follow in a tradition of 180 years' duration, that began on April 30, 1789, in New York City with the inauguration of General George Washington.

It has been said that politics stops at the water's edge. Perhaps it should also be said that politics stops at high noon of Inauguration Day. For at the moment the President takes the oath of office he becomes not the President of a political party or of a particular viewpoint, but the President of all Americans. He symbolizes the process of orderly change, of rededication and self-renewal, which is the genius of our system.

Thus, with tremendous challenges visible in every direction, it was particularly appropriate in this year of 1969 that President Nixon set a theme of "Forward Together." For surely, it behooves every man of goodwill to strive for unity at this moment and go forward in a cause larger than one's self.

As another Chief Executive pointed out many years ago, the President takes an oath to preserve, protect, and defend the Constitution of the United States. But in so doing, he assumes the solemn obligation which every citizen must also share with him.

"The Constitution which prescribes his oath, my countrymen, is yours; the government you have chosen him to administer for a time is yours; the suffrage which executes the free will of men is yours; the laws and the entire scheme of our civil rule, from the town meeting to the state capitols and the national capitol, is yours."

So said Grover Cleveland in his Inaugural Address of March 4, 1885. They are words worth pondering in 1969.

And so we on the Inaugural Committee have been especially sensitive this year to the nature of our times. We have, in the concert, the festive balls, the receptions, parade, and gala, sought to recapture the gaiety which characterizes this still-young, still-growing nation.

We have sought also to express, through word and deed, the affirmative spirit of America—knowing that this is a time once again to engender that common purpose, that spirit of unity which has carried us over the shoals and crevices of the past.

As chairman of the 1969 Inaugural Committee, it has been my privilege to serve at this time of high drama and importance. I hope that the activities of Inaugural Week marked just the beginning of a new era of united purpose.

My deep appreciation goes out to all members of the Inaugural Committee and to the hundreds of volunteers, as well as the many thousands who were our guests here in Washington, D.C.

It is my hope that this handsome volume, *The Inaugural Story*, will preserve this moment in history and, by its contents and its tone, serve as a record of what we have done and as a reminder of what we have pledged to do.

Let the spirit of the inauguration carry us "Forward Together."

J. Willard Marriott, Chairman

W. Peale   delin.

The First Inauguration

When the new republic of the United States began to make preparations to inaugurate its first President in 1789, there was nowhere to turn for advice or guidance. Not only were American precedents totally lacking, but there were no foreign examples to follow, for the idea of a nation with a President who governed by the will of the people was a novel one to most of the world. The problem was further complicated by the character of the President-elect—for George Washington was no ordinary man. He was as towering a hero as this nation has ever had, and there were many who talked of making him king instead of merely President.

Thanks both to Washington's dignity and sense of fitness and to the basic democratic instincts of those responsible for conducting the inauguration, the ceremony in which the first President was sworn into office was simple and restrained. However, the people insisted on acclaiming Washington, as Americans have always demanded the right to honor their heroes, and the homage he received before and after the inauguration was full and heartfelt.

That first inauguration, at the corner of Broad and Wall streets in New York City, set a precedent for all those that would follow. The scene has changed completely in 180 years, the trappings are more lavish, and thirteen states have now become fifty, but the swearing-in of Richard Nixon on the portico of the Capitol in Washington in 1969 was not basically different from that of George Washington on the balcony of New York's Federal Hall in 1789. Here Francis Russell, a historian who writes of the period, describes that first inauguration and some of the events leading up to the moment when Washington placed his hand on an open Bible and swore a solemn oath.

A festooned Gray's Ferry (really a floating bridge) on the Schuylkill greeted Washington on his way to New York.

13

The ramshackle toll bridge across the Schuylkill River at Gray's Garden outside Philadelphia was owned by the brothers G. and R. Gray, and in honor of its passage by the first President of the United States the brothers had concealed the rickety sides with cedar branches and erected a laurel arch at either end. A row of banners fluttered along the bridge's north side—one for each of the eleven states that had ratified the Constitution—while the flag of the American Union stood alone midway on the south side. Flags lined the approach. One proclaimed "The New Era"; another displayed an enormous liberty cap with the familiar, if scarcely appropriate, warning "Don't Tread on Me"; still others expressed the wish that Commerce might flourish, or displayed the rising sun of empire.

Not unaware of the publicity value of patriotism, the brothers Gray had spared neither money nor ingenuity, even arranging to have a small girl perch on the near arch and drop a laurel wreath on General Washington's brow when he passed beneath her. Fortunately both for her reputation for accuracy and the General's equanimity, the brothers developed second thoughts. As Washington, on his splendid white horse, rode under the arch, the child merely lowered the wreath until it hung just above his head. Austerely elegant in buff and blue, unobservant of the suspended laurels, the President-elect clattered across the uneven planks and onto the Philadelphia road. It was the morning of April 20, 1789, bright and spring-like.

Four days before, Washington had left Mount Vernon by coach for his New York inauguration. He was accompanied by a former aide, Colonel David Humphreys, and by the secretary of Congress, Irish-born Charles Thomson, who had brought him the formal notification of his unanimous election as the first President of the United States. To the retired General, only recently recovered from a severe attack of rheumatism, Thomson's arrival was more expected than welcome. During the years of the Revolution, through all the exigencies and frustrations of command, Washington had quietly fixed his mind on a future day when he could lay aside his sword and return to Mount Vernon, and here among his green acres he was at last able to make a reality of his long-held dream. If his country could thenceforth get along without him, so much the better for himself and Mount Vernon. But the foundering coalition of the thirteen states could not. Whether the Union with its newly adopted Constitution and its new Congress would endure or fall apart seemed to depend on General Washington.

Washington was indeed the father figure, more revered and honored than loved familiarly, a republican with the dignity of a monarch, standing above shifting opinions and party strife, a symbol for *all* Americans. Many people have followed the Pied Piper lure of a seeming father figure to their ruin, but Washington was truly what he seemed—the embodiment of selfless duty. Since his duty was so apparent, he must and would accept the unanimous offer of the electors to become the first President.

He would infinitely have preferred tending his acres for the span that the Great Watchmaker had allotted him to directing the uncertain destiny of the emergent nation. Even financially he felt the pinch, for he was land-poor, and the lavishness of Mount Vernon's hospitality strained his resources. On agreeing to accept the electors' offer, he borrowed five hundred pounds to discharge his debts and then had to borrow a hundred more for his expenses to New York. Before setting out on his journey, he wrote to his bluff old companion-in-arms General Henry Knox: ". . . in confidence I tell you, with the *world* it would obtain little credit, that my movements to the chair of government will be accompanied by feelings not unlike those of a culprit who is going to the place of his execution; so unwilling am I, in the evening of a life nearly consumed in public cares, to quit a peaceful abode for an ocean of difficulties, without that competency of political skill, abilities and inclination which is necessary to manage the helm. I am sensible that I am embarking by the voice of the people, and a good name of my own, on this voyage; but what returns will be made by them, Heaven alone can foretell. Integrity and firmness are all I can promise."

What happened as the coachman cracked his whip and the coach drew away from Mount Vernon, what the men said to one another, were not recorded, but Washington in his diary noted his own depression. He found its converse in the jubilant mood of his countrymen waiting to greet him along the way. For the future of the Union with its new Constitution and Congress seemed assured with the old Commander in Chief at the helm. At Wise's Tavern in Alexandria, in the first of a succession of such festivities, the mayor and leading citizens gave him a dinner at which thirteen toasts were drunk and he was extolled as the "best of men and most beloved fellow-citizen."

Washington tried to cover the maximum distance in a day, starting every morning at sunrise and traveling until evening, and he soon found the zeal of his escorts a hindrance to a speedy journey. He spent the first

Washington salutes welcoming Trenton citizens in this primitive painting.

night at Spurrier's Tavern, a little over twelve miles from Baltimore, where the city's volunteer artillery welcomed him the next day with a roar of cannon. After a supper with some of his former officers at the Fountain Inn, he listened to more complimentary addresses, which were becoming repetitious. At ten he was in bed, and by half past five was once more in his coach. An unsensational two-day journey through a thinly settled countryside brought him to Wilmington just after sunset. The next morning Wilmington's burgesses and common council made their formal address to him, which he had managed to see informally beforehand in order to prepare a reply. Another escort of eager, hampering gentlemen rode beside his departing coach.

At the Pennsylvania boundary waited a new guard of honor, composed of members of the Pennsylvania assembly and the City Troop of Horse, smart in white breeches, high-topped boots, and round black hats bound with silver. Washington left his coach to mount the white stallion that they had brought for him. The party breakfasted at Chester at the early hour of seven. After making a brief speech, Washington rode on at the head of an ever-lengthening column until he came to the laurel arches of Gray's Garden.

The dusty main road from the bridge was lined with people. Washington, in his blue coat, passed with grave grace, bowing constantly to the shouts and handclaps of the spectators. As he neared the city, cannon boomed, church bells rang, and the ships anchored in the Delaware ran up all their flags. Twenty thousand applauding Philadelphians stood by to watch him ride down Market and Second streets to City Tavern. There leading citizens had arranged a great dinner for him to which "all the clergy and respectable strangers in the city" were invited.

Seventy-five miles still lay ahead, a distance that could be covered in two and a half days if the weather held out and there were not too many speeches along the way. Before Washington left Philadelphia the next morning under an overcast sky, he had to listen to five more addresses. He did manage, however, to persuade the City Troop not to escort him to Trenton. A light rain began to fall as the coach moved across the placid Delaware countryside, where the Continental Army had once marched so painfully. Just before Trenton, at the bridge over the Assunpink Creek, where Washington had faced the British on a desperate afternoon twelve years before, a group of women and girls with flowers in their hair waited to sing an ode in his honor. Behind them the bridge was masked by an arch of greenery

against which hung a banner with the date of Trenton's liberation and the words "The Defender of the Mothers will also Defend the Daughters." The female voices concluded their ode:

Strew, ye fair, his way with flowers—
Strew your Hero's way with flowers.

As the last couplet echoed, little girls with baskets of flowers pushed forward to scatter blossoms in the General's path. Bowing deeply and obviously moved, Washington thanked them for the great honor done him. In the evening, after a public dinner, he found time to write—in the third person—thanking the young ladies for the "affecting moment" at the bridge. The next morning he was off again at sunrise with a Trenton escort that rode with him the eight miles to Princeton, where he had breakfast. He was met at almost every town by the mayor and a group of leading citizens, and the inevitable address followed to the accompaniment of cannon and church bells. At Elizabethtown, where he was to embark for New York, the whole population seemed to have gathered at the water front. Before the brief harbor voyage on the ceremonial barge awaiting him, the General reviewed a detachment of militiamen drawn up on the dock.

That barge, prepared and paid for by forty-six prominent New Yorkers, had a forty-seven-foot keel, a mast and a sail, and places for a crew of thirteen oarsmen. New York pilots had vied for the honor of rowing in the new President. They, with the coxswain, wore white smocks and fringed black caps. After admiring the barge, Washington embarked, followed by a joint committee of Congress and dignitaries of the city government of New York. Not until midday did the barge pull away from the pier, the artillery firing salutes from the shore while the troops on the water front stood at self-conscious attention. With sail and oar in a following wind the presidential party moved swiftly across Newark Bay and past Staten Island.

Approaching Upper Bay, the oarsmen changed their stroke. In that larger reach of water a sloop under full sail bore down on them, and as she closed, Washington heard the familiar melody "God Save the King" sung to new words honoring him. From a smaller boat a male chorus rendered an ode in harmony, and one of the seagoing choir managed to hand the coxswain some printed copies. To complete the festive progress, porpoises began playing around the barge's prow. As the brisk wind whipped the barge forward, the southern tip of New York grew clearer, and soon the masses lining the water front from the fort to the end of Wall Street became distinguishable as individuals.

Old enmities forgotten, a British packet at anchor south of Governor's Island fired a salute of thirteen guns, which was answered almost at once by an American battery. Not to be outdone, a nearby Spanish vessel broke out the flags of a score of countries and dispatched a fifteen-gun salute. Among the ever-growing flotilla in the wake of the barge was the schooner *Columbia*, commanded by the Revolutionary poet Philip Freneau and laden with a cargo of African monkeys.

In New York all work had stopped. Everyone whose legs could carry him was at the water front to see General Washington's barge arrive at Murray's Wharf, at the foot of Wall Street. Three huzzas were given with vigor as the cannon of the Battery fired their welcoming salute. The barge docked at about half past two. So great was the ensuing din that even the pealing bells were drowned out. Washington, in his wig and three-cornered hat, looking as stylized as a rococo porcelain figure, walked down the gangplank with slow, stately steps and up a flight of carpeted stairs, its rails hung in crimson velvet. He was met by Governor George Clinton and a crowd of officials. A self-important officer commanding the guard of honor saluted the General and announced that he awaited orders. Washington thanked him, then, turning to the crowd, added: ". . . after this is over, I hope you will give yourself no further trouble, as the affection of my fellow-citizens is all the guard I want."

So dense was the throng at Murray's Wharf that the planned parade could not get started. When at last the guard had forced a narrow way to the waiting coach, it took Washington a half hour to move the ten-minute distance from the dock to Franklin House, his assigned residence. Not even Franklin House—previously used by the president of Congress and now refurbished for the President of the United States—offered him sanctuary from importunate well-wishers. He had not time to change his clothes before Governor Clinton's coach was back at the door to take him to the inescapable honor banquet. Before the toast-ridden dinner ended, rain was again falling, but even that did not dampen the fireworks display that the weary General was forced to applaud before gaining the refuge of his bedroom.

The next morning Washington assured a joint committee of Congress that any arrangements made for his induction into office would be acceptable. Congress promptly voted to inaugurate him on April 30. During the intervening six days he was so overwhelmed with

John Adams, pictured above in a study for a portrait by John Copley, began presiding over the Senate on April 21, a week before Washington was inaugurated, and took up much of that time with such questions as whether Washington should be called "His Majesty," "His Highness," or "His Elective Highness," and whether the senators should stand during Washington's Inaugural Address.

Overleaf: Washington's crossing of New York Harbor from New Jersey to the Battery was a triumphal one, saluted by flag-decked, cannon-firing ships all along the way. However, the artist has left the President-elect's barge somewhat undermanned, for all accounts tell that it was rowed by thirteen oarsmen, one for each of the states.

visitors at Franklin House that Mount Vernon in retrospect seemed a hermitage. "I was unable to attend to any business whatsoever," he admitted later. Meanwhile Congress was debating a proper title for the incoming President. John Adams, with a non-Puritan affection for dynastic trappings, favored "His Most Benign Highness." The Senate preferred "His Highness, the President of the United States of America, and Protector of the Rights of the Same." Fortunately for posterity, the representatives, goaded by the sharp tongue of the Pennsylvania frontier democrat William Maclay, determined on having nothing more than was set down in the Constitution: "President of the United States." Washington wanted no title at all.

Inauguration Day was announced at sunrise by thirteen guns of the Battery. Washington dressed with unusual care in a new suit of brown American-made broadcloth that had been woven at Hartford and that was set off by metal buttons stamped with the American eagle. His hair was powdered, and he wore the customary white silk stockings and silver shoe buckles. Although the joint committee of Congress would not arrive before noon to escort him to Federal Hall, crowds began to gather hours earlier in front of Franklin House, festive in the April sunshine, their holiday mood made more solemn by the measured ringing of church bells. At the committee's arrival, militiamen lined up in the roadway and forced the crowd back. Washington entered the ornate coach-and-four provided for him by Congress, his hat in his hand, a dress sword in a steel scabbard at his side, his Inaugural Address tucked into a special inner pocket of his new suit. Preceded by dragoons, artillerymen, and grenadiers in all the gay contrasts of their dress uniforms, the presidential coach, with a coachman on the box and a lackey on one of the horses, moved through the banner-decked and cheering streets to Federal Hall on Wall Street, where the two houses of Congress awaited their President.

Congress was already assembled in the Senate chamber, a square, classical room draped in crimson damask,

its ceiling decorated with a sun and stars. Vice President John Adams stepped forward to welcome Washington formally on his arrival while legislators and their guests rose from the semicircle of seats. To Adams' formal question as to whether he would take the oath, Washington replied that he was ready to proceed. The Vice President conducted him across the room and through a triple doorway to a porticoed balcony overlooking Wall Street. On the balcony stood an armchair and a red-draped table on which lay a velvet cushion holding the large Bible belonging to St. John's Masonic Lodge of New York. There, in the open air, with two of his old generals and a few other guests standing by him, Washington took the oath of office.

New York's Chancellor Robert R. Livingston administered the oath, which Washington repeated, his hand on the Bible: "I do solemnly swear that I will faithfully execute the office of President of the United States and will, to the best of my ability, preserve, protect, and defend the Constitution of the United States." "I swear, so help me God," Washington added in his grave voice; he then bent forward and kissed the book. With a broad gesture toward the crowd, Livingston shouted: "Long live George Washington, President of the United States!" In a surging roar the crowd took up the cry, cheer after cheer billowing through the streets, with one repeated identifiable phrase: "God bless our President." The new flag was raised above Federal Hall's cupola, and as it fluttered brightly from the staff, the guns of the Battery responded in salute while the cannon of anchored ships boomed and church bells pealed.

Amidst the congratulatory din Washington stood quietly in his brown suit of American cloth, bowing acknowledgment, the recognized embodiment of the new nation. Those cheering in the streets as well as those gathered in the hall felt the uncertainty about the future replaced by confidence through his presence. Already they were calling him the Father of his Country. By the grace of Washington, Americans were assured that the new nation would endure.

This old engraving of Washington's inauguration on the balcony of Federal Hall in New York City was made from a drawing by an eyewitness. The ceremony was held outside so the huge crowd could see it, but the Inaugural Address was given inside only to Congress. The precedent of outdoor inaugurations did not begin until Andrew Jackson took his first-term oath on the Capitol portico in 1829.

21

Spires of the Spirit

The Inaugural gala festivities this year, in their faith and hope for the future, brought memories of long ago when another Chief Executive who was both a General and a President stood at the Capitol steps for his second term of office.

Less than a decade after the close of the War Between the States, the elected head of the indivisible Union came to his second inaugural. With great renown won on the fields of battle, in campaigns to preserve intact the Republic, he became the 18th President. His name—Ulysses S. Grant. The Inaugural Ball of 1873 was staged in a huge 330-foot structure erected for the occasion in Judiciary Square. The interior decorations were spectacular. A unique feature for the gala night was the placing of several hundred caged canaries inside the great hall. These feathered songsters, in their yellow vestments, were counted on to lift rapturous cadences above the chords of the Marine Band salute, "Hail to the Chief."

But it all turned out to be a chilly illustration that the best-laid plans of mice and men—or, shall we say of birds and men—oft go awry. For not a canary contributed a note to the expected presidential oratorio. Each of the hundreds of singing birds was utterly mute because every member of that golden-surpliced choir was utterly miserable. The trouble was that every contingency had been thought of in the arrangements with the exception of the weather. On that March day the temperature was near zero. That polar setting stifled songs.

The songless canaries, with their padlocked throats and their frozen melodies, suggest a parable that every loyal citizen of the democratic wonder we call America ought seriously to take to heart.

The solemn fact is that every real American is given the opportunity to help create the atmosphere in which, in spite of jibes and lies, democracy can really sing. In a government where the people rule, a part of that "singing air" is constructive, kindly criticism, which has its eye upon the next generation rather than on the next election. In the free air of our dear land every man has the right to his opinion and the right to freely express it. He even has the right to be wrong.

All the worth of criticism depends upon the spirit in which it is made. If one's voice is to help engender an atmosphere in which democracy can sing, it must not, with ugly insinuations, question the patriotism and sincerity of those who differ. It must be fair and sincere. If a fellow American disagrees with another without being disagreeable, then all is well. The canaries of mutual cooperation for the total good, not of a party, but of the nation, will sing on Inauguration Day.

The unpardonable sin of citizenship is to sit on the sidelines in the seat of the scornful, oblivious to the terrible toll the heaviest office in the world takes from any man who occupies the White House. God pity little souls, devoid of human kindness, who have nothing but cutting, bitter criticism for any attempt of the administration in power to guide the ship of state through turbulent seas with false lights on the shore.

Let us remember that inaugural hopes never can sing in the freezing atmosphere of unreasoning prejudice, blind partisanship, and mean criticism. To so change the nipping air by the warmth of our own kindly understanding and cooperation that one silent songster, huddled in the cold, will throw back its drooping head and pour out notes of confident joy because we came near, is the richest satisfaction earth can give.

A thermometer simply registers the temperature. A thermostat can change it. Blessed is the man who looks for what he can commend rather than for what he can condemn, who warms the frosty hostile air, whose kindly cadences keep men on their feet.

Dr. Frederick Brown Harris   Former Chaplain, United States Senate

Inaugural Committees, Yesterday and Today

George Washington's inauguration in the City of New York, in 1789, was followed by a fireworks display. It is possible that the first Inaugural Committee was created to manage that event. The first functioning Inaugural Committee in the District of Columbia may have been created to direct the special illumination of the City of Washington following Thomas Jefferson's first inauguration, in 1801.

"The citizens of Washington have arranged for and provided for all the pomp and circumstance that has marked these occasions," stated the *Official Souvenir Program* of the inauguration of 1901. Certainly the citizens of Washington were active in inaugural ceremonies as early as 1841, when a group of "Managers of the Inaugural Ball" was composed of prominent local residents. Records show that, as early as 1873, the residents of the city appeared to be in full control of arrangements for the inaugural festivities. A leaflet issued by the 1873 Inaugural Committee states that "the committees appointed by the citizens of the metropolis" were arranging the events which had by that time become traditional. Inaugural activities that year included the parade, fireworks, illuminations of public and private buildings, and the Inaugural Ball.

Since 1873 the basic organization of an Inaugural Committee and several subcommittees has steadily grown. The 1969 Presidential Inaugural Committee comprises some thirty-two subcommittees which manage the myriad functions incident to the inauguration. However, the present committee, like all of its predecessors, does not include the administration of the oath of office to the President-elect and Vice President-elect within its activities. That constitutional requirement is executed by Congress and the Chief Justice. A Senate Committee of Arrangements directed the ceremony before 1901, and since that date a joint congressional Committee on Inaugural Ceremonies has arranged the administration of the oaths of office.

While the citizens of Washington made up the Inaugural Committee of 1873 and those of other years, it is not clear whether or not those committees were of a partisan political nature. However, in 1893 the Democratic National Committee appointed the "General Committee," which took charge of the inaugural ceremonies. The chairman of the National Committee of the President-elect's party appointed chairmen for the inaugural committees from 1901 to 1913. Inaugural committees were thus quite political during that period.

The nonpolitical nature of inaugural committees ensued by 1940. Congressional resolutions of that year, and of 1944 and 1948, provided that the chairmen of inaugural committees would be appointed *with the approval* of the President-elect. Since 1948, the chairman of each Inaugural Committee has been appointed *by* the President-elect. In most recent years, the appointment of the chairman and establishment of the inaugural committees has been accomplished pursuant to the provisions of the Presidential Inaugural Ceremonies Act of 1956 (70 Stat. 1049). This act precludes inaugural committees from being creatures of political parties. Such committees are, both in law and in practice, nonpartisan groups charged with creating appropriate ceremonies for the inauguration of our Chief Executives.

The 1969 Presidential Inaugural Committee is a microcosm of our nation. Proud Americans from every facet of our society, committed individually and mutually to this quadrennial duty, have gathered to honor the man and the theme . . . "Forward, Together."

Philip C. Brooks, Jr.   Historian-Archivist of the Inaugural Committee

Mrs. George Aiken, the Vermont senator's wife and a Book and Program Committee member, checks first run of the program with Robert K. Gray, committee chairman. Below, Robert G. McCune, Inaugural Committee executive director.

Above, Chairman Marriott and his wife (right) talk to workers.

The Inaugural Committee at Work

The entire procedure of the inauguration of a President—and hence the work of the Inaugural Committee—rests on tradition. For the Constitution merely prescribes the words of the oath of office that the President-elect must take. From this simple requirement a three-day celebration has evolved, which every four years renews the patriotism and national pride of a democracy, ordinarily devoid of pomp and ceremony. In the process of evolution, the Inaugural Week activities have become something more meaningful to the American people than the celebration of a political victory.

The thousands of volunteers comprising the Inaugural Committee had little more than two months between the election and the inauguration in which to stage the national extravaganza that transcends all political and class divisions in the United States. For this reason the committee sought out all interested citizens, regardless of political party, to volunteer their time and effort to the huge task.

With the appointment of the Inaugural Chairman, the 1969 Inaugural Committee began to take shape. Following guidelines established by Inaugural Committees of previous years, the various committees were appointed to organize and direct the individual events. Within a matter of days the entire 1969 committee was organized, staffed, housed, and ready to plan, promote, and stage the traditional activities that Americans have come to expect with the installation of a new President.

Home for the Inaugural Committee was the old Pension Building (the site of Grover Cleveland's first Inaugural Ball in 1885, and of every other Inaugural Ball through that of Taft in 1909). By the time the first of the thirty-two major committees was ready for action, the interior of the building had been transformed with bunting, streamers, and posters. The army of volunteers who worked through the long days and late into the nights brought the scene to life. At any one moment the committee at work as viewed from the second-floor balcony of the building was like an impressionistic painting of blurred colors with heavy daubs of red, white, and blue. Add to this the volume and acoustical reverberations of Grand Central Station for the sound. Then throw in the action of an old Keystone Cops movie for the motion. All combined—inaugural psychedelia.

The workers ranged from very young to very old, every one of them eager to do all he could. They worked toward, and by turns they anticipated, dreaded, prayed for, and feared January 20, 1969. They drew blueprints, painted posters, held press conferences, stuffed envelopes, and drank gallons of coffee. They were reminded of the days remaining, like shopping days till Christmas, by a crudely painted sign suspended above the maze of temporary office dividers. And throughout it all, they were rewarded from every corner and every pillar with the grateful smiles and approving eyes of the President- and Vice President-elect.

The various committees were chaired by distinguished party leaders, business men and women, and people outstanding in other fields, all of whom donated time and services. Most had never worked on an inauguration before. But with their committee members the chairmen often worked around the clock, and when the makeshift chronometer indicated one day to go, the floats had been finished, the grandstands erected, the ballrooms decorated, the official program printed, and the concert sold out.

In this manner, over the years, the Inaugural Ceremonies have been transformed into much more than the cold and simple formality of inducting a man into office. They have become events shaped by the people to whom they belong. As a political rite they stand as a symbol of the inner harmony of our government. As a tradition, the Inaugural Ceremonies eloquently testify that in America the people are sovereign.

F. C. Duke Zeller

Above, a session of the Book and Program Committee in progress in the Old Pension Building.

Above, Mrs. Jack Miller (left), wife of the senior senator from Iowa, and Mrs. John Tower, wife of the senior senator from Texas, look over documents during one of the many meetings they attended. At right, a press conference held by the Inaugural Ball Committee.

Mrs. Wayne R. DeLaney, Inaugural Committee accountant.

1969 INAUGURAL COMMITTEE

J. Willard Marriott, Chairman
Robert G. McCune, Executive Director

CHAIRMEN OF COMMITTEES

ARMED SERVICES PARTICIPATION
Maj. Gen. Charles S. O'Malley, Jr., Chairman

BUDGET
W. Leslie Douglas, Chairman
Webb C. Hayes III, Co-Chairman

CIVIC PARTICIPATION
William H. Press, Chairman

CONCERT
Mrs. Marjorie Merriweather Post, Honorary Chairman
Hon. S. Dillon Ripley II, Chairman
Mrs. Carl L. Shipley, Co-Chairman

CONCESSIONS
Berkeley G. Burrell, Chairman

CONGRESSIONAL LIAISON
Douglas Whitlock, Chairman

DECORATIONS
Leon Chatelain, Jr., Chairman

DISTINGUISHED LADIES' RECEPTION
Mrs. Dwight D. Eisenhower, Honorary Chairman
Mrs. J. Willard Marriott, Chairman
Mrs. C. Wayland Brooks, Co-Chairman

FINANCE
Robert C. Baker, Chairman

GOVERNORS' RECEPTION
Maj. Gen. George Olmsted, Chairman
Robert W. Fleming, Co-Chairman

GRANDSTANDS
Lt. Col. Sam D. Starobin, Chairman

HOSPITALITY
Harold D. Fangboner, Chairman
Mrs. Harold D. Fangboner, Co-Chairman

HOUSING
Donald S. Bittinger, Chairman

INAUGURAL BALL
Mark Evans, Chairman
Mrs. Leslie C. Arends, Co-Chairman

INSURANCE
G. Dewey Arnold, Jr., Chairman

LAW AND LEGISLATION
F. Elwood Davis, Chairman

MEDALS
Dr. Melvin M. Payne, Chairman

At the right, Edward R. Carr (right), chairman of the Parade Committee, and Robert A. Collier, a committee vice chairman, visit the unfinished reviewing stand.

Putting together an inaugural means countless committee meetings and phone calls, plus reminders of what it is all for.

Youth or age, to be served, give of themselves in causes they believe important.

Below, Franklin W. Roskelley of the Central Correspondence System revises the sign he posted daily to January 20.

MEDICAL CARE AND PUBLIC HEALTH
Dr. Milton C. Cobey, Chairman
Dr. William Cooper, Co-Chairman
Henry S. Robinson, Jr., Co-Chairman

PARADE
Edward R. Carr, Chairman

PROGRAM AND BOOK COMMITTEE
Hon. Robert Keith Gray, Chairman

PUBLICITY
Fred B. Morrison, Chairman

PUBLIC SAFETY
Chief John B. Layton, Chairman

RELIGIOUS OBSERVANCE
Judge Boyd Leedom, Chairman
Rabbi A. Nathan Abramowitz, Co-Chairman
Rt. Rev. William F. Creighton, Co-Chairman
Rabbi Harry J. Kaufman, Co-Chairman
Rev. Graydon McClellan, Co-Chairman
His Eminence Patrick Cardinal O'Boyle, Co-Chairman
Pres. Milan D. Smith, Co-Chairman
Rev. Charles L. Warren, Co-Chairman

SPECIAL GROUP PARTICIPATION
Earl Kennedy, Co-Chairman
Rev. Martin J. McManus, Co-Chairman
Celso Moreno, Co-Chairman

SPECIAL SERVICES
William Armstrong, Chairman

STATE SOCIETIES
Lewis E. Berry, Chairman

TRANSPORTATION
William Calomiris, Chairman

UNITED CITIZENS
Michael Gill, Chairman
All American Gala:
Gen. Emmett O'Donnell, Jr., Chairman
Mrs. John S. D. Eisenhower, Co-Chairman

VETERANS PARTICIPATION
Edward F. McGinnis, Chairman

VICE PRESIDENT'S RECEPTION
Hon. Louise Gore, Co-Chairman
Charles S. Bresler, Co-Chairman

VOLUNTEERS
J. R. Pat Gorman, Chairman

YOUNG REPUBLICANS
Jack McDonald, Co-Chairman
Dottee Fancher, Co-Chairman
Ben Cotten, Co-Chairman

EXECUTIVE VICE CHAIRMEN
Hon. John Clifford Folger
Hon. Perkins McGuire
Jack Drown

Volunteers in the Old Pension Building prepare invitations for mailing.

Mark Evans, chairman of the Ball Committee (standing, above), meets with volunteers.

Above, Mrs. Leslie Arends, Ball Committee co-chairman and wife of the House minority whip, discusses arrangements for the ball with the press. Below, Mrs. Claire Lee Chennault (behind table), special advisor to the Inaugural Committee chairman, answers queries on press credentials.

VICE CHAIRMEN
Carl L. Shipley
Mrs. J. Willard Marriott
Gilbert Hahn, Jr.
Hon. Howard Jenkins, Jr.
Hon. Walter E. Washington
Bruce J. Terris
John H. Sharon

HONORARY VICE CHAIRMEN
Edward H. Foley
Dale Miller

TREASURER
L. A. Jennings, Treasurer
Robert E. Kragh, Associate Treasurer
James E. O'Neill, Associate Treasurer

COMPTROLLER
James A. Councilor, Jr., Comptroller
Mrs. Edna Nick, Assistant Comptroller
Mrs. La Verne E. Pinkerton, Executive Assistant to Comptroller
Mrs. Wayne R. DeLaney, Accountant

GENERAL COUNSEL
Robert W. Barker

ASSOCIATE GENERAL COUNSELS
Herbert E. Marks
R. Richards Rolapp

SPECIAL ASSISTANTS TO THE CHAIRMAN
John M. Christie
William J. McManus

EXECUTIVE ASSISTANT
Mrs. Mervel Denton

EXECUTIVE SECRETARY
Mrs. Dolores Smith

STAFF SECRETARIES
Mrs. Eunice Larson
Miss Shirley Massenburg
Mrs. Angela Raisch
Mrs. Dorothy Sparks

ADMINISTRATIVE ASSISTANTS TO THE CHAIRMAN
Philip C. Brooks, Jr., Historian-Archivist
Mrs. Claire L. Chennault, Special Advisor
Hon. Clement E. Conger, Protocol
Robert C. Diefenbach, Radio and TV Consultant
Capt. Warren K. Hendriks, Jr., Military Aide
Mr. and Mrs. M. Belmont Ver Standig, Promotion Consultants

LIAISON OFFICERS
John D. Ehrlichman, for the President
Arthur J. Sohmer, for the Vice President
Douglas Whitlock, for the Joint Congressional Committee
Josephine L. Good and William S. Warner,
    for the Republican National Committee

Mr. Nixon displays a victory present from Julie: the Great Seal done in crewelwork.

The Presidential Family

Richard Milhous Nixon spent sixteen years training for the Presidency. They were years of deep commitment, years in which he sifted the many problems of the Presidency, searching for answers of the mind and heart.

Eight of those years were spent as the hardest-working Vice President the nation had known. Eight more were spent out of office, while Mr. Nixon applied himself with equal vigor—sometimes during periods of personal disappointment, to build for causes larger than himself.

Today it is clearly evident that his energies in those years were wisely invested, for the new President has taken hold of this most difficult of offices with virtuosity. His calming manner, his measured tones have provided the prime national force in lowering voices of stridency, which have been prevalent in recent years.

Yet the professionalism of his manner did not prevent him from taking strong steps early in his Presidency. With no need for further apprenticeship, Richard Nixon undertook an eight-day trip in Europe when he was barely six weeks into his term of office and thus marked himself as a President capable of using the surging tide of world events to national advantage. He moved successfully through six European capitals, reaffirmed old friendships, strengthened new ones. He evidenced a poise and confidence that certified Richard Nixon had arrived as a world leader and was fully comfortable in the role.

Within days of this trip, he opened the Presidency to

Pat Nixon and daughter Julie share a happy moment, above. At right, Tricia Nixon, Dwight David Eisenhower II, Mamie Eisenhower, and Julie—married December 22, 1968, to David—were photographed during the Vice President's reception at the Smithsonian Institution. Tricia, 22, quiet and pretty, graduated in June, 1968, from Finch College in New York. Twenty-year-old David, the competent and self-assured grandson of the former President, is a junior at Amherst. His spritely wife, also 20, is a junior at nearby Smith. The young couple lives off-campus in Northampton, Massachusetts.

the people on the subject of foreign affairs. In this most difficult of presidential problem areas, the new President spent a full hour on national television discussing with the people questions of the most serious import. Without notes, without hesitancy or evasion, he responded to questions on which a slip of the tongue could have damaged the international rapport he had achieved. His answers in this performance gave evidence of the seasoned experience of the new President, evidence that he grasps the global consequences of his leadership and recognizes the primacy of his role.

There have been other glimpses of Mr. Nixon's solid preparation for the Presidency. The man whose television appearance may have cost him the office in 1960 has emerged in 1969 as a master of this all-pervasive medium.

As millions have seen on television, he is today a man of serious and steadfast purpose, yet a President with a gift of laughter, including the ability to laugh at himself.

Mr. Nixon's long preparation for the Presidency goes back to 1952. During the campaign of that year, General Dwight D. Eisenhower promised that, if elected, he would make an operating office of the Vice Presidency and would school his running mate in the complexities of the Presidency. When he followed through on this political promise, Eisenhower found he had an apt and eager pupil.

It was Mr. Nixon's good fortune to serve under a President who believed in exercising his right hand, and he performed each assigned task with a poise and skill that invited more of the same. By presidential order he attended all Cabinet, National Security Council, and legislative meetings. There were no secrets between the Chief Executive and his Vice President.

Representing the President overseas, the Vice President visited fifty-four nations, covered more than 160,000 miles outside the United States. He had extended discussions with thirty-five presidents, nine prime ministers, five kings, and two emperors.

During those vice-presidential years, Mr. Nixon had heavy responsibilities at home, as well. At one time he worked all through Christmas week at his own home to bring about settlement of a nationwide steel strike. He presided at more than 11 per cent of all Cabinet meet-

ings during his Vice Presidency and established himself in the minds of those who saw him operate as a man of unusual powers—indefatigable, keenly analytical, yet open and warm.

Those who had the opportunity to sit with him at the Cabinet table came to note Mr. Nixon's alert reactions to the variety of problems laid before the Chief Executive. There was opportunity to note the respect with which others at the Cabinet table—all but one older than he—listened and heeded his counsel and advice. In the middle of a heated discussion among his colleagues, Vice President Nixon often moved in to clarify a point, interpret congressional action, or ask just the right question to draw out the full facts from his colleagues to keep their discussions headed to a purposeful end.

Tireless then as now, it was common to see him arrive at the White House for a 7:30 A.M. meeting after he had been at a protocol or diplomatic function the night before. He seemed always to have the energy, and somehow found the time, to read the briefs, make the speeches, see the people, and write the letters required, and still get to meetings on time. His attendance record at Cabinet meetings was nearly perfect, even during political campaigns.

He has met the many demands of public life unstintingly, yet wisely he has not allowed his own family life to be sacrificed in the process. Through two decades in the national spotlight, the Nixons have reared two remarkably poised and devoted children. The strength of this closely knit family has only rarely been glimpsed by Americans, but it is there—a significant factor in the life of the President.

Here, then, is Richard Nixon, our 37th President. He is a mainstream American, forged in the crucible of public life, whose story has been one of continuing growth and continuing commitment. He can lead because he can inspire. He can teach because he himself is still a student. He is a man in whom is entrusted many hopes, a man on whom an entire world now counts for those certain trumpet notes of leadership.

Robert Keith Gray
Secretary of the Eisenhower Cabinet

Portrait
of the
Vice President

$\mathcal{S}$piro Theodore Agnew is a diligent and dedicated individual, possessing qualities that the President saw months ago. He is a man of energy and one quick to learn, a man of dignity and common sense. He knows that every journeyman is first an apprentice, and that the path to success requires steady work. The Vice President has impressed all of us in the Senate by taking his job as President of the Senate as seriously as the Constitution intended, and it is obvious that he has spent exhausting evening hours studying the Senate rules and learning the intricacies of our parliamentary procedure.

These attributes were molded into his character early in the Vice President's life. President Nixon has said of Spiro Agnew, "He has experienced poverty and prejudice and risen above them on his own merits." Born in Baltimore in 1918, the son of Greek-American parents, he knew many hardships as a young man and learned the necessity of hard work and industry. He

The Agnew family, left to right: Susan, 21; the Vice President's wife, Judy, who was married to Mr. Agnew, then an Army lieutenant, in 1942; in her lap Mrs. Agnew holds granddaughter Michelle Ann; Pamela, 25; J. Rand, "Randy," 22; Kimberly, 13; the Vice President; and Randy's wife, mother of Michelle Ann, the former Ann Herbert.

Sparkling and pert, Elinor Judefind Agnew, pictured at the right in her Inaugural Ball gown, has been called Judy since her Forest Park High School days in Baltimore. Born in Baltimore, the daughter of a chemist, she met Spiro Agnew when they were both employed at the Maryland Casualty Company. The two eldest Agnew girls, Pamela and Susan (below) are actively involved in public service—Pamela as a social worker, Susan as secretary to a staff member for the minority leadership in the Congress.

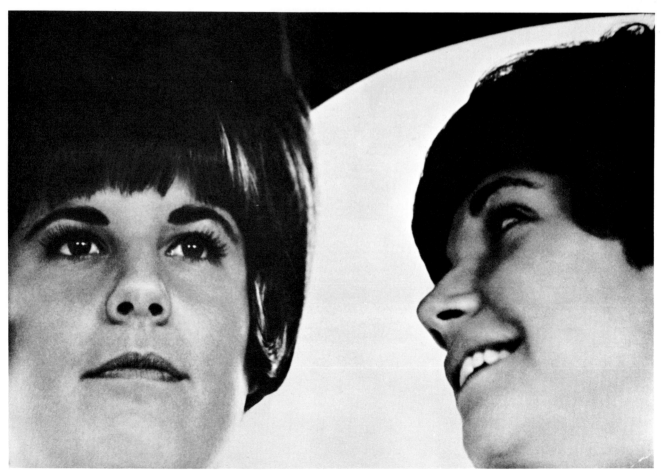

worked in a food market, sold insurance, and taught night school while working his way through law school. During World War II, he married Elinor Isabel (Judy) Judefind, the daughter of a Baltimore chemist.

Vice President and Mrs. Agnew have four children and one granddaughter. Pamela, 25, is a social worker in Baltimore County, Maryland. Randy, 22, is married and is the father of the Vice President's grandchild, 18-month-old Michelle Ann. Just back from ten months' duty in Vietnam with the Seabees, Randy and his wife reside in suburban Washington, while he attends the University of Maryland. The next Agnew child, Susan, 21, is a secretary on Capitol Hill, while Kimberly, 13 and the youngest, attends the National Cathedral School in Washington.

Spiro Agnew brings to the Vice Presidency the point of view of a man in tune with middle-class America. As a former governor and county government official, Mr. Agnew has been in contact with citizens on an eye-to-eye basis and knows their problems and their concerns. Because of his recent experience at local government levels, he tends to look at the federal structure from the bottom up, concerned with the ways such programs touch people.

He brings to his new office a willingness to respond, a keen and inquiring mind, coupled with the ability to listen to the other view. It is a combination of characteristics that enables him to obtain a ready rapport with those he meets. A quick and friendly smile, together with his legal training and experience as both a county and state executive, indicate both compassion and good humor.

Because of his experience in dealing with the facets of urban life, Spiro Agnew brings a special knowledge of the complex problems that confront our metropolitan areas. He has emerged as a new leader in the encouragement of urban redevelopment and rehabilitation and is aware of the need to re-establish the rule of law as a prerequisite to making cities livable again.

In short, he is a pragmatist, not a dogmatist, a man qualified by experience and natural bent to work for the betterment of people in one of the crucial areas of American life, the urban level. Though his new duties require him to attend to many jobs, ranging from presiding over the Senate to hosting diplomatic functions, Spiro Agnew's heart remains with the people.

It can truly be said that the Office of Vice President is certain to grow with the man who now occupies it.

George Murphy   United States Senator

Unlike the standard image of the baby-kissing politician, the Vice President (above with his winsome granddaughter) really likes—and communicates naturally with—children.

Hail and Farewell

arred by only a few exceptions, Inauguration Day traditionally has been a festive one in the United States, a day of real or affected camaraderie between incoming and outgoing Chief Executives. The spotlight belongs to the new President; and on the whole, departing leaders have grasped the fact and stepped aside gracefully. True, Theodore Roosevelt appeared to attract more attention than his hand-picked successor, but not through design: Roosevelt was a flamboyant, colorful figure who dominated any scene of which he was part; he didn't steal the show so much as William Howard Taft, reserved and somewhat standoffish, characteristically gave it up. Similarly—such problems seem to be peculiar to Presidents who chose their own successors—Andrew Jackson was the principal object of interest at Martin Van Buren's inauguration. As Senator Thomas Hart Benton put it, "For once the rising was eclipsed by the setting sun."

If Inauguration Day belongs in the main to the new President, it has not always been clear which of the two leaders on the podium was the happier. John Adams, who was practically paranoid about the necessity of his having to follow the larger-than-life Washington as President, thought he heard his predecessor say, "Ay! I am fairly out and you fairly in! See which of us will be happiest!" And if Washington didn't say it, he probably thought it. Just after James Madison took the oath of office, someone commented to the newly liberated Thomas Jefferson, "You have now resigned a heavy burden." "Yes, indeed," Jefferson replied, "and am much happier at this moment than my friend." As he delivered Abraham Lincoln to the White House in the troubled year 1861, the long-suffering James Buchanan left his successor with these words: "If you are as happy, my dear sir, on entering this house as I am leaving it and returning home, you are the happiest man in this country." And Taft, too, who had said of the Presidency, "I'll be damned if I am not getting tired of this," outsmiled Woodrow Wilson in 1913 as he almost gratefully turned over the reins of government.

Congeniality is difficult when the President and President-elect belong to different political parties; for some incumbents who have been defeated by their successors, it has been impossible. (Taft's magnanimity was an exception, not the rule.) Indeed, the first two Chief Executives to be denied second terms by the electorate refused even to attend the inauguration that would end their tenure. Of course, both of the defeated Presidents happened to be named Adams, which meant that they were sensitive, jealous, and tended to take rejection very, very personally. The third defeated incumbent, Martin Van Buren, did not attend William Henry Harrison's swearing-in; but he had, despite a particularly bitter election campaign in 1840, made a point of calling on and receiving Old Tippecanoe during the interregnum. Having been informed that President-elect Grant would not ride in the same carriage with him, President Andrew Johnson declined to attend the inauguration of 1869. His vindictive feelings toward the government and the Senate that had impeached him did not last long, however, and in 1875 he returned to Washington as a United States senator. (With John Quincy Adams, Johnson was the only former President to return to elected national office; Adams was a congressman for the last seventeen years of his life. Taft returned to government in nonelective capacities and in 1921 was appointed Chief Justice of the Supreme Court by President Warren Harding.) Haggard, partially paralyzed, and dying, Woodrow Wilson accompanied Harding to the Capitol on Harding's Inauguration Day but could not go outside in the cold March weather to witness the ceremonies.

Presidential boycotts of the inauguration have been rare, however, and most departing leaders were able to bring themselves to make the trip from White House to Capitol with their successors. John Tyler, who had assumed the Presidency with sureness and strength on the death of Harrison, had wanted and been denied renomination by his party. Nevertheless, despite his bitter disappointment, he behaved with selfless dignity in 1845: on Inauguration Day he directed his carriage to stop at the National Hotel and pick up President-elect James Polk, whom he escorted to the Capitol. Polk was extremely courteous to Tyler and attempted to be gracious to his own successor (Polk chose not to seek reelection), General Zachary Taylor. He gave a lavish dinner for the new administration shortly before the inauguration, but found Taylor to be "exceedingly ignorant of public affairs, and . . . of very ordinary capacity." Benjamin Harrison and Grover Cleveland twice took the inaugural drive together, exchanging roles: Harrison's election in 1888 interrupted Cleve-

Tradition once had it that Jefferson rode a horse to his inauguration (arriving, left). In fact, he walked. John Adams did not see his successor's swearing-in but, after finishing some last-minute tasks, left the city before dawn. Below, President Grant and President-elect Rutherford B. Hayes leave the White House for the Capitol in March, 1877.

The Daily Graphic, MARCH 9, 1877

Taft and Wilson (above, riding to the 1913 ceremony) corresponded chattily about presidential life before the inauguration. Among other tips, Taft assured Wilson that the financial burdens were light and recommended the retention of two members of the White House staff who had served the Tafts well. At right, Truman and Eisenhower in 1952.

land's two terms. When Cleveland left office in 1897, he literally had to lean on McKinley's arm as the two men entered the Senate chamber: the outgoing Democrat was suffering from gout and had to attend the inauguration of the Republican with one shoe off.

In 1933, after a twelve-year Democratic famine and in the middle of a depression, the atmosphere between new and passing administrations was not even cordial. Herbert Hoover and Franklin Roosevelt took the auto ride from White House to Capitol together, but they scarcely glanced at one another or conversed along the way: the whole thing was an embarrassment to both. Not until twenty years later was there opportunity for two Presidents to make the trip together, when President-elect Eisenhower and President Truman rode down Pennsylvania Avenue to the Capitol. However, the two men had had a long record of close cooperation, beginning in the closing months of World War II, when General Eisenhower was in command of Allied Forces in Western Europe and Truman had become President, and resuming again when the General be-

came Supreme Commander, North Atlantic Treaty Organization. The working relationship between the two had more often than not been smooth and cordial, and if their recent political rivalry had created any strain between them, it was not apparent to those who watched them ride by together.

Inauguration Day is the new President's day; and petty differences are out of keeping with the spirit of the occasion. Although the most recent inaugurations involving a new and old President have seen a change in the party of the Chief Executive, the ceremonies have been conducted with the greatest dignity and in the spirit of cooperation. President Eisenhower handed the office to President Kennedy not in the spirit of Republican to Democrat, but of one generation to the next. And in 1969, two men who had been political opponents for two decades rode from the White House to the Capitol in an obvious mood of sharing: what one had experienced, the other was about to experience— the terrifying burden of the world's most difficult and important job.

*Dwight D. Eisenhower and John Kennedy journeyed to-
gether to the Capitol with the change in administration in
1961, but it was not the last meeting of the two men, for the
young President continued to call on the General from time
to time for advice. At left, the two confer at Camp David
in 1962 during the tense days of the Cuban missile crisis.*

*Posing for photographers before their ride together down
Pennsylvania Avenue to the Capitol on Inauguration Day,
Lyndon Johnson and Richard Nixon displayed a mutual
respect and good humor as they chatted amicably about inaugural weather and the Johnsons' dog Yuki. The scene
was symbolic of a tone they had labored to set during the
past months. For President Johnson, the orderly transfer
of power had begun with his decision not to seek a second
full term. As the major candidates for his job entered the
lists, he conferred with them from time to time in an attempt
to keep the campaign from seriously rocking the ship of
state. And although Nixon frequently commented that the
country could have but one President at a time, once he was
President-elect there was apparent a partial blending of
the outgoing and incoming administrations—a conscious
superimposition of the two men and their aims—for the
period of transition. They had different styles and points
of view; they had opposed each other often. But now, as in
recent months, they reflected the shared interests of Americans—a spirit Nixon capsulized as, "Forward together."*

47

Inaugural Week Schedule

RECEPTION FOR DISTINGUISHED LADIES
Saturday, January 18   National Gallery of Art, 2 to 5 p.m.   By Special Invitation

YOUNG AMERICA'S INAUGURAL SALUTE
Saturday, January 18   Washington Hilton, 4 to 7 p.m.   By Special Invitation

THE INAUGURAL ALL-AMERICAN GALA
Saturday, January 18   National Guard Armory, 9 p.m.   Tickets Available to Public

GOVERNORS' RECEPTION
Sunday, January 19   Sheraton Park Hotel, 2 to 5 p.m.   By Special Invitation

RECEPTION HONORING THE VICE PRESIDENT-ELECT AND MRS. SPIRO T. AGNEW
Sunday, January 19   Smithsonian Museum of History and
Technology, 5 to 8 p.m.   By Special Invitation

INAUGURAL CONCERT
Sunday, January 19   Constitution Hall, 8:30 p.m.   Tickets Available to Public

OFFICIAL INAUGURAL CEREMONY
Monday, January 20   The Capitol, 11:30 a.m.   By Special Invitation

INAUGURAL PARADE
Monday, January 20   2:00 p.m.   Tickets Available to Public

INAUGURAL BALL
Monday, January 20   9:00 p.m.   By Special Invitation

Inaugural Ceremony

PROGRAM
East Portico, National Capitol   11:30 a.m. January 20, 1969

Invocation
by the Right Reverend Charles Ewbank Tucker

"God Bless America"
by the United States Marine Band

Prayer
by Rabbi Edgar F. Magnin, D.D.

The Oath of Office will be administered
to the Vice President
by the Honorable Everett McKinley Dirksen

Prayer
by His Eminence Iakovos

"This Is My Country"
by the Mormon Tabernacle Choir

Invocation
by the Reverend Dr. Billy Graham

The Oath of Office will be administered to the President
by the Chief Justice of the United States

Four ruffles and flourishes, "Hail to the Chief,"
and 21-gun salute

Inaugural Address
by the President of the United States

"The Star-Spangled Banner"
by the Mormon Tabernacle Choir and the
United States Marine Band

Benediction
by Archbishop Terence J. Cooke

At the burned-out Capitol, James Monroe is sworn in by Chief Justice John Marshall.

"The Unity
That
Keeps Us Free"

*W*ith malice toward none, with charity for all, with firmness in the right, as God gives us to see the right, let us strive on to finish the work we are in, to bind up the nation's wounds. . . ." Perhaps the most familiar of all Inauguration Day phrases, these words of Abraham Lincoln also reflect the most characteristic of all Inauguration Day sentiments—conciliation, the quest for national unity. Like any great nation, the United States often has been divided. Our national elections have tended to stress these divisions. But the inauguration of a new President has served the important quadrennial function of restoring unity and stressing the wholeness of the country.

The precedent was established the first time the highest office in the land changed hands. Although he was ill-equipped by nature to be a healer, John Adams nevertheless assumed the role in his Inaugural Address. Winner of the first seriously contested presidential election, "His Rotundity" was nervous and overconscious of being dwarfed in stature and presence by General Washington. But after Chief Justice Oliver Ellsworth administered the oath of office, Adams dedicated himself to work for a reconciliation of "various political opinions . . . and virtuous men of all parties. . . ."

Still, disharmony became the hallmark of the Adams administration, and the spirit carried through to the election of 1800. Although Thomas Jefferson was elected by the House of Representatives only sixteen days before his March 4, 1801, inauguration (he had tied with Aaron Burr in the electors' votes), the new Chief Executive liked to call his victory the "Revolution of 1800." The Federalists, fearing the democratizing effects of Jeffersonian leadership on the American government,

agreed with the terminology. Appointed Chief Justice in the twilight of Adams' term, John Marshall faced the prospect of swearing in Jefferson with distaste: "Today," he wrote on the morning of the inauguration, ". . . the new order of things begins . . . it is not difficult to foresee that much calamity is in store for our country. . . ." Yet Jefferson's speech placated even the headstrong Marshall. Calling for a restoration of "harmony and affection without which liberty and even life itself are but dreary things," Jefferson reminded his audience that "every difference of opinion is not a difference of principle. We have called by different names brethren of the same principle. We are all Republicans, we are all Federalists."

But, as Marshall and Jefferson both demonstrated, conciliation was not the only theme of inaugurations. The ceremony represented the victory of one party and set of principles over another. And so there was an undercurrent at many swearings-in, of triumph on one hand and, on the other, of fear and dismay at what the new President might do. Nine times Marshall administered the oath of office, and to five Presidents—Jefferson, Madison, Monroe, John Quincy Adams, and Jackson; all but Adams were politically obnoxious to the Chief Justice. At Madison's second inauguration, according to one story, the imposing Federalist jurist stared at the tiny Chief Executive—whom Washington Irving had called "a withered little apple-John"—with such scorn and disgust that Madison blushed.

Andrew Jackson did not achieve the Presidency by stressing national harmony; he was the champion of the common man, the representative of farmers and laborers against the privileged, moneyed, big-city classes.

And his inauguration was a celebration of the common man's victory. "I have never seen such a crowd here before," said Daniel Webster wryly. "Persons have come five hundred miles to see General Jackson, and they really seem to think that the country is rescued from some dreadful danger!" Backwoodsmen, dock workers, smiths, and small-time merchants swarmed into Washington, sleeping five in a bed or on billiard tables, and patronized stores that sold Jackson-style cravats and barbers that gave Jackson-style haircuts. "It was like the inundation of northern barbarians into Rome," noted one observer, ". . . and every face seemed to bear defiance on its brow." "The reign of King MOB," said Supreme Court Justice Story, "seemed triumphant." "The country is ruined past redemption," lamented John Randolph of Virginia.

It wasn't, of course. But the Jacksonian image remained stamped on the Presidency and its occupants for decades. Indeed, in order to regain the office, the opposition consolidated into the Whig party and in 1840 nominated a rough-hewn military man, William Henry Harrison, hero of Tippecanoe. In the famous "log cabin and hard cider" election campaign that year, "Old Tip" easily won. At his inaugural on March 4, 1841, Harrison insisted on continuing in the role of rough-and-robust military man. Despite bitter, damp, gale-driven cold, he declined to go to the Capitol in a carriage but rode horseback without an overcoat or hat, and then delivered the longest Inaugural Address in history: it lasted nearly two hours. Unfortunately, unlike many men called old-one-thing-or-another, Old Tip was really old (sixty-eight), and the exposure, added to the strains of preparing an administration, proved too much for him. Exactly one month to the day after taking the oath of office, he died.

John Quincy Adams commented that through death William Henry Harrison was "taken away thus providentially from the evil to come." The evil was the division of the United States—an ever-widening schism between North and South, abolitionists and moderates, secessionists and compromisers. In their Inaugural Addresses, incoming Chief Executives (and they were always new—after Jackson, no President was re-elected until Lincoln) attempted to stress union and deplore divisiveness. Polk promised to be the President of "the whole people of the United States." Zachary Taylor pledged to "assuage the bitterness which too often marks unavoidable differences of opinion." Franklin Pierce, in a strikingly eloquent address that was the first inaugural delivered from memory, pleaded for ac-

ceptance of compromise, warning the people that "beautiful as our fabric is, no earthly power or wisdom could ever reunite its broken fragments." "Time is a great corrective," said James Buchanan, asking an end to agitation on the slavery issue and pointing out that sectional jealousy and hostility involves "all in one common ruin."

But words could not heal then. The inaugurals of Presidents from Polk to Lincoln might be conciliatory and reasonable, but partisans were not, and even Presidents gave signs they thought unreason had the upper hand. In his first Inaugural Address, Abraham Lincoln, having slipped into Washington secretly because of threats to his life, spoke to the South as well as the North when he said, "We are not enemies, but friends. . . . Though passion may have strained it must not break our bonds of affection." But he was clear, too, that the issue would be faced. "In *your* hands, my dissatisfied fellow-countrymen, and not in *mine*, is the momentous issue of civil war." The conflict did come; before it was over, in his second Inaugural Address, Lincoln was already asking an end to malice, for the application of charity, for the closing of wounds. Yet he was angrily opposed, even by members of his own party, and then a madman's malice ended his life.

The calls for unity from Reconstruction Presidents were virtually meaningless. The conciliatory words needed the support of conciliatory actions from at least one side. Ironically, it was Rutherford B. Hayes, whose disputed election threatened to bring on armed conflict again, who strengthened the appeal for oneness. "I call upon you," Hayes said in his 1877 inaugural, ". . . fellow citizens, here and everywhere, to unite with me in an earnest effort to secure to our country the blessings . . . of justice, peace, and union—a union depending not upon the constraint of force, but upon the loving devotion of a free people." And then he effectively put an end to "carpetbagger" rule in the South and removed federal pressure for Negro rights.

Although unity has been the dominant theme of inauguration speeches, few Presidents between the Civil War and very recent times directed themselves in those speeches to racial as well as sectional unity; the issue was too sensitive and, at the same time, not yet fully joined. One who did was James A. Garfield, the Ohio Republican who had once been an evangelist preacher. In his 1881 Inaugural Address he accurately forecast the problems that America some day would face if it ignored the situation. Universal education for all, Garfield said, was the key to the future; in its interest, "sections and races should be forgotten." Our children, he said, "will surely bless their fathers . . . that both races were made equal before the law."

For now, these were fond hopes only. Yet by the 1880's American Presidents were regaining from Congress the control over issues that Jackson had had but that had since been denied the office because of the basic and terrible divisions within the nation. The American style of life was changing fast. The country was being drawn into world politics. Problems were less local, more national. The equilibrium in the two-party system had been restored, giving back meaning to the national democratic process.

Grover Cleveland's 1885 inauguration was the Easter of the Democratic party, which had not had one of its own inaugurated at the Capitol in twenty-eight years. Cleveland celebrated by delivering his address without benefit of a manuscript. "God, what a magnificent gambler!" said Senator John Ingalls. The new President stuck to the old unity script: "Today the executive branch of the Government is transferred to new keeping. But this is still the Government of all the people."

Four years later Cleveland left the White House, no longer a bachelor. On the Inauguration Day of his successor, Benjamin Harrison, Cleveland's young bride remarked to one of the servants, "I want you to take good care of all the furniture and ornaments in the house, for I want to find everything just as it is now when we come back again. . . . We are coming back just four years from today." And they did.

Cleveland's second successor, William McKinley, was the first President to be exposed to the Inauguration Day malady known as Theodore-Roosevelt-steals-the-show. In 1900, Roosevelt had been nominated for the Vice Presidency mainly with the intent, on the part of the bosses, to *take* him from the public eye, not to place him in it. The first sign that the plan would not be successful was the response to the incoming Vice President at the inaugural in 1901. In the parade, the lion's share of the applause was for the Rough Rider.

In 1905, Theodore Roosevelt himself was taking the oath of office, and for the second time. The plan to kick T.R. upstairs and out of sight backfired six months after the 1901 inaugural, when McKinley was assassinated. Roosevelt transformed the office—particularly after he had won his own resounding victory in 1904. His brief, direct Inaugural Address in 1905 spoke of unity—but largely in terms of a national dedication to making those changes that the times required. It was

notable, for example, in that Roosevelt did not promise to "avoid foreign entanglements"—a pledge that had become standard to Inauguration Day rhetoric. "We have become a great nation," the President said, "forced by the fact of its greatness into relations with the other nations of the earth, and we must behave as beseems a people with such responsibilities." Roosevelt was the first President who seemed to comprehend fully the implications of science and technology in the modern world. "Modern life is both complex and intense, and the tremendous changes wrought by the extraordinary industrial development of the last half-century are felt in every fiber of our social and political being." Without mentioning the forgers of trusts and monopolies by name—or even by class—the President implied that regulation of corporate capitalism had become a foremost responsibility of government: "If we fail, the cause of free self-government throughout the world will rock to its foundations, and therefore our responsibility is heavy, to ourselves, to the world as it is to-day, and to the generations yet unborn."

William Howard Taft was in many ways a progressive in conservative's clothing, a believer in traditional means to accomplish progressive ends. Taft's Inaugural Address, though long and sometimes ponderous, actually was a courageous definition of his not-at-all uniformly popular aims. Like T.R., he favored "federal supervision and restriction" of big business, "the conservation of our resources," an activist foreign policy calculated "to promote peace . . . to defend our interests and assert our rights with a strong hand." Taft also asked for an end to "outbursts of race feeling among our people against foreigners," who were still emigrating to America in huge numbers; and for the enforcement of the Fifteenth Amendment, which guaranteed the voting rights of Negroes, and which had "not been generally observed in the past. . . . We are charged with the sacred duty of making their [the Negroes'] path as smooth and easy as we can."

The American people, Roosevelt and Taft both seemed to say, elected their President to lead. He might sometimes lead them into new roads, but in any

Overleaf: The gay spirits and light clothing shown in this view of William H. Harrison's inaugural belie that day's bitter weather, which helped lead quickly to Harrison's death by pneumonia. Daniel Webster joked that in editing the Inaugural Address—rich in historical references— he had "killed seventeen Roman proconsuls as dead as smelts," but it still took nearly two hours to deliver.

Illustrated London News, 1845

Above, the crowd collects in the rain for Polk's inaugural. On the platform Samuel F. B. Morse tapped out the first "live" play-by-play account of a swearing-in, for the benefit of listeners in Baltimore. Evidently, Polk's was the first inaugural at which "Hail to the Chief," an ancient Scottish air, was performed—then as now by the Marine Band.

event he would need the support of their best natures in order to lead. This theme would appear in many subsequent inaugurals.

Probably the most intellectually gifted President since Thomas Jefferson, Woodrow Wilson defied the traditional legend that said that Americans were inherently anti-intellectual. Without abandoning his scholarly, almost stuffy bearing, he had become a man of the people, exuding trust in them because he did trust them, and they, him. At the inauguration, a cordon of guards kept the area in front of the podium clear. Rising to take his oath, Wilson said to a guard, "Let the people come forward." Those words became the real Inaugural Address and the watchwords of the Wilson administration.

As though ominously, the wind blew so hard and so shrill at Wilson's second inaugural that almost no one heard him speak, and few applauded at the end. Yet this was Wilson's real call to the American heart: the United States, he said, alluding to the Great War across the Atlantic, believed that "the essential principle of peace is the actual equality of nations in all matters of right or privilege; . . . peace cannot securely or justly rest upon an armed balance of power."

To be "true to ourselves—to ourselves . . . and in the thought of all those who love liberty and justice . . ."—Wilson was asking America to become the conscience of mankind, and it was too much to ask, just then. Four years later, his own dream of a League of Nations that would end all war broken, his own body broken and mind periodically dulled from the effects of a stroke, Wilson was assisted from the Senate while, outside, Warren G. Harding inaugurated a different kind of era:

"America, our America, the America builded on the foundation laid by the inspired fathers, can be a party to no permanent military alliance. It can enter into no political commitments, nor assume any economic obligations which will subject our decisions to any other than our own authority. . . . This is not selfishness, it is sanctity. It is not aloofness, it is security. It is not suspicion of others, it is patriotic adherence to the things which made us what we are."

"Our supreme task," Harding said, repeating a campaign theme, "is the resumption of our onward normal way." Times had changed, and with them the norm. But the body politic was exerting its periodic check upon its leadership.

In 1933 the nation was in trouble; half the people foresaw little opportunity; millions were homeless and distrustful of the system that had brought them this Depression. The future was dim; hope had been replaced by fear.

As though to emphasize that his administration would need apolitical help if it were to lift the nation from its troubled state, President-elect Franklin Roosevelt—in a then private gesture that has since become traditional—led his Cabinet to St. John's Episcopal Church on Inauguration Day for morning prayer. Later, after taking the oath of office from Chief Justice Charles Evans Hughes, the new President turned to the crowd before him—and to the radio microphones he mastered so effectively.

"This is preeminently the time to speak the truth, the whole truth, frankly and boldly. . . . This great nation will endure as it has endured, will revive and will prosper. So, first of all, let me assert my firm belief that the only thing we have to fear is fear itself—nameless, unreasoning, unjustified terror which paralyzes needed efforts to convert retreat into advance." Roosevelt defined the causes of the crisis, suggested remedies, made it clear that the government would try almost anything. "We face the arduous days that lie before us in the warm courage of the national unity. . . . We do not distrust the future of essential democracy. The people of the United States have not failed. In their need they have registered a mandate that they want direct, vigorous action. They have asked for discipline and direction under leadership. They have made me the present instrument of their wishes. In the spirit of the gift I take it." By his fourth inaugural, when America was at war, no cries for unity were necessary. The country was whole again; "Dr. New Deal" had been replaced by "Dr. Win-the-War"; and as a national healer and unifier, the latter was most effective. With the end of the war new potential issues of division were springing up right and left. Yet, strangely—to his opponents not much less than to his supporters—whatever had to be done would have to be done without Roosevelt. He had been President for so long, and through such diverse and trying times, that it was difficult to adjust to the Presidency without him.

But there, in 1949, before the Capitol, reading and hardly ever looking up from the manuscript into the television cameras, was Harry Truman, the "average man" whom few could accept after F.D.R.'s death, and who was not supposed to have won the election of 1948. There he stood, the apotheosis of middle America, not only proclaiming isolationism dead, but offering our "store of technical knowledge" to all peace-loving nations; offering to "foster capital investment in areas needing development"; and out-Wilsoning Woodrow Wilson by asserting, "Only by helping the least fortunate of its members to help themselves can the human family achieve the decent, satisfying life that is the right of all people."

The world was as turbulent as it had been after World War I; and in contrast to America's inactivity abroad then, the nation seemed to be involved everywhere. This new role was difficult to understand, and real and imagined threats from abroad and from within created a current of uneasiness and fear in the United States. There was no man better equipped to reassure the nation in its unfamiliar new posture than the one who took the oath of office in 1953.

"We sense with all our faculties that forces of good and evil are massed and armed and opposed as rarely before in history," said President Eisenhower after being sworn into office by Chief Justice Fred Vinson: "At such a time in history, we who are free must proclaim anew our faith. . . . Freedom is pitted against slavery; lightness against the dark. . . . We must be willing, individually and as a Nation, to accept whatever sacrifices may be required of us. . . . Patriotism means equipped forces and a prepared citizenry. Moral stamina means more energy and more productivity, on the farm and in the factory. Love of liberty means the guarding of every resource that makes freedom possible —from the sanctity of our families and the wealth of our soil to the genius of our scientists. . . ."

Eisenhower guided the United States through a tumultuous period while maintaining a national atmosphere of placidness. By 1960, however, a younger America, its memory of hot war dulling, its patience with cold war diminishing, looked to a different sort of leadership, appropriate for a different sort of time.

"Let the word go forth from this time and place," announced John Kennedy in 1961, voicing the new attitude, "to friend and foe alike, that the torch has been passed to a new generation of Americans—born in this century, tempered by war, disciplined by a hard and bitter peace, proud of their ancient heritage—and unwilling to witness or permit the slow undoing of those human rights to which this Nation has always been committed, and to which we are committed today at home and around the world." In an appeal to the nation's allies and competitors, Kennedy asked for new explorations of differences, formulations of "precise proposals" for arms control, exchanges of arts and trade, cooperation in space ventures. "All this will not be finished in the first 100 days. Nor will it be finished

in the first 1,000 days, nor in the life of this administration, nor even perhaps in our lifetime on this planet. But let us begin."

Kennedy was murdered, and within a year, Lyndon Johnson had been given his own mandate—by an unprecedented 61 per cent of the popular vote—to continue to seek the aims of Kennedy's New Frontier, which, in the Johnson version, became the Great Society. Fittingly, at the 1965 inauguration, Johnson began his address not with a plea for national unity, but with a statement that the nation was in fact united:

"My fellow countrymen, on this occasion, the oath I have taken before you and before God, is not mine alone, but ours together. We are one nation and one people. Our fate as a nation and our future as a people rest not upon one citizen, but upon all citizens." Asserting that modern times had created a world in which "there are possibilities enough for all who will abandon mastery over others to pursue mastery over nature," the President asked for rejection of "any among us who seek to reopen old wounds and to rekindle old hatreds. They stand in the way of a seeking nation. . . . For the hour and the day and the time are here to achieve progress without strife, to achieve change without hatred —not without difference of opinion, but without the deep and abiding divisions which scar the union for generations."

There is something remarkable, indefinably effective about the inauguration as a tool of healing, even though the cure may not itself be long-lasting. It is as if Americans learn again, each four years, that they are one people, and are grateful for the event. Four years after Lyndon Johnson had received his record-breaking mandate, the nation was wounded, torn by strife and hatreds, old and new, scarred by its deep divisions. But the year ended, and a new year began, and twenty days later a new President spoke to his countrymen and to "my fellow citizens of the world community:

"I ask you to share with me today the majesty of this moment. In the orderly transfer of power, we celebrate the unity that keeps us free."

An instant made the nation whole. The wounds were bound; only time would tell if they were healed.

With the unfinished Capitol dome as a brooding backdrop and in an emotional atmosphere suffused with premonitions of tragedy, Abraham Lincoln took the oath of office in March, 1861. Overleaf: President Dwight D. Eisenhower's second swearing-in was held on the kind of gray-tinged day that Americans have come to associate with an inaugural.

OVERLEAF CREDIT: UPI

To ensure the dignity of the inauguration, Congress in 1905 provided that thenceforth a Joint Inaugural Committee of three senators and three representatives should be in charge of planning all events in connection with the ceremony of swearing in the President at the Capitol. The members of the committee in 1969 were:

Senator Everett M. Dirksen of Illinois, Chairman; Senator Mike Mansfield of Montana; Senator B. Everett Jordan of North Carolina; The Speaker of the House, John W. McCormack of Massachusetts; Representative Gerald R. Ford of Michigan; and Representative Carl B. Albert of Oklahoma.

This committee was assisted by a staff of six. Its members were:

J. Mark Trice, Secretary of the Senate Minority, Executive Director; William Brownrigg III and William S. Cheatham, Assistant Directors; and Dorothy M. Burns, Jeanne G. Dorrance, and Robert P. Meredith.

The Significance of the Inaugural Ceremony to the American People

Senator Dirksen and J. Mark Trice of the Joint Inaugural Committee

The Inauguration Ceremony of 1969 was probably viewed by more people in more places than any other inaugural in the history of the nation. Television has given ringside seats to the inaugural to millions of people who could not possibly be accommodated within the geographical limits of the District of Columbia.

The millions of dollars of television time and the utilization of the most sophisticated tools of the communications media would not be so massively deployed were not the events reflected therein of the most widespread interest to the American people as well as to the people throughout the world.

The significance of the event taking place can be evaluated by the official positions of those present. The outgoing President and Vice President. The new President and Vice President. The Chief Justice of the United States and the members of the Supreme Court. The members of Congress are present. The diplomatic corps and dignitaries of high rank from all walks of life.

President Nixon reflected this significance when, in his opening remarks he addressed, "My fellow citizens of the world community: I ask you to share with me today the majesty of this moment. In the orderly transfer of power, we celebrate the unity that keeps us free.

"Each moment in history is a fleeting time, precious and unique. But some stand out as moments of beginning, in which courses are set that shape decades or centuries. This can be such a moment."

Indeed, the Inaugural Ceremony is the distillation of democracy in action. It has been preceded by many months of the most concentrated activity by groups of people and individuals engaged in an assiduous and determined advocacy of political principles and personal campaigning for the confidence and support of the voters of the United States.

The campaigns are conducted as thoroughly and carefully as resourceful and imaginative human minds can devise, to attract the maximum public attention to the candidates. It is entirely appropriate then, that when the people have made their choice that the transfer of governmental responsibility take place publicly, and with the dignity and solemnity commensurate with the investiture of leadership "of the people, by the people, for the people."

The inauguration is visible and demonstrative public evidence of the unity of the people of this great nation of ours and of the continuity of orderly patterns of government. One party wins and the other party loses. The losers are however no less important to the fabric of government. They are as responsible as every other American for the success of our form of government and like every other American must work hard to advance the national interests of the United States and of all its people.

The title of these remarks, "The Significance of the Inaugural Ceremony to the American People," impels one to consider further the solemnity of the occasion. An oath is taken by the new President, a formal invocation of the witness of Almighty God to the sincerity of purpose of the President, as he places his hand on the open pages of a Bible. Clergymen are present to invoke the blessing of the Creator on the people of the United States and on the men they have chosen to be their leaders, that this nation may prosper, in justice and in righteousness. It is evidence of the fact that this is not an irreligious nation and that we mean what we say when we refer to the blessings of liberty.

Too, it can scarcely have escaped notice that the oath of office is administered by the Chief Justice of the Supreme Court of the United States. With some rare exceptions this has become traditional although the Constitution contains no provision to specify the officer or individual who is to administer the oath. The Supreme Court had not been appointed at the time of President Washington's first inauguration and the oath was administered to him by Chancellor Livingston.

At Washington's second inaugural Chief Justice John Jay was abroad on official business and the oath was administered to him by Associate Justice William Cushing of the Supreme Court. The second President of the United States, John Adams, was the first one to have the oath of office administered by the Chief Justice. Oliver Ellsworth, who had been instrumental in fashioning the legislation to establish the Supreme Court, was the Chief Justice to achieve that distinction.

The vitality of our tripartite system of government, a coequal representation of the legislative, executive, and judicial branches, is manifested by this ceremony taking place as it does on the steps of the Capitol with the House of Representatives on one side and the Senate on the other.

The Inauguration Ceremony is a highly visible, symbolic affirmation of faith in our concepts of self-government, of modern progress, of our faith in God and our sensitivity to the wisdom of the ancients. Pliny the Younger declared many hundreds of years ago, "The prince is not above the laws, but the laws above the prince."

Because it quite properly belongs to the people, the ceremony traditionally takes place out of doors, in the midst of the people who are the real rulers of this great country and whose leaders and representatives exercise their authority "by the consent of the governed." This is the true and enduring significance of the Inaugural Ceremony to the American people.

Everett McKinley Dirksen
United States Senator

The 1969 Inaugural Ceremony

The 37th President takes the oath of office, his right hand resting on two open Bibles held by his wife. The leather-covered Bibles have been handed down for generations in the Nixon family: one was printed in 1828, the second in 1873. Both are opened to the second chapter of Isaiah, fourth verse: "And he shall judge among the nations, and shall rebuke many people: and they shall beat their swords into plowshares, and their spears into pruning hooks: nation shall not lift up sword against nation, neither shall they learn war any more." Mr. Nixon used the same passage in both his inaugurations as Vice President.

The Nixons and the Agnews stand together at the lectern as the spectators applaud and their predecessors smile.

Above, the two principals chat with the out-going President and Vice President. Below, Mrs. William P. Rogers, wife of the Secretary of State (with her leg in a cast), and Mrs. Clifford M. Hardin, wife of the Secretary of Agriculture, in the Capitol Rotunda on their way to the Inaugural Ceremony.

Pat Nixon, Judy Agnew, and Lady Bird Johnson, all stylishly wrapped against the cold.

President Nixon's Inaugural Address

Senator Dirksen, Mr. Chief Justice, Mr. Vice President, President Johnson, Vice President Humphrey, my fellow Americans—and my fellow citizens of the world community:

I ask you to share with me today the majesty of this moment. In the orderly transfer of power, we celebrate the unity that keeps us free.

Each moment in history is a fleeting time, precious and unique. But some stand out as moments of beginning, in which courses are set that shape decades or centuries.

This can be such a moment.

Forces now are converging that make possible, for the first time, the hope that many of man's deepest aspirations can at last be realized. The spiraling pace of change allows us to contemplate, within our own lifetime, advances that once would have taken centuries.

In throwing wide the horizons of space, we have discovered new horizons on earth.

For the first time, because the people of the world want peace, and the leaders of the world are afraid of war, the times are on the side of peace.

Eight years from now America will celebrate its 200th anniversary as a nation. Within the lifetime of most people now living, mankind will celebrate that great new year which comes only once in a thousand years—the beginning of the third millennium.

What kind of a nation we will be, what kind of a world we will live in, whether we shape the future in the image of our hopes, is ours to determine by our actions and our choices.

The greatest honor history can bestow is the title of peacemaker. This honor now beckons America—the chance to help lead the world at last out of the valley of turmoil and onto that high ground of peace that man has dreamed of since the dawn of civilization.

If we succeed, generations to come will say of us now living that we mastered our moment, that we helped make the world safe for mankind.

This is our summons to greatness.

I believe the American people are ready to answer this call.

The second third of this century has been a time of proud achievement. We have made enormous strides in science and industry and agriculture. We have shared our wealth more broadly than ever. We have learned at last to manage a modern economy to assure its continued growth.

We have given freedom new reach. We have begun to make its promise real for black as well as for white.

We see the hope of tomorrow in the youth of today. I know America's youth. I believe in them. We can be proud that they are better educated, more committed, more passionately driven by conscience than any generation in our history.

No people has ever been so close to the achievement of a just and abundant society, or so possessed of the will to achieve it. And because our strengths are so great, we can afford to appraise our weaknesses with candor and to approach them with hope.

Standing in this same place a third of a century ago, Franklin Delano Roosevelt addressed a nation ravaged by depression and gripped in fear. He could say in surveying the Nation's troubles: "They concern, thank God, only material things."

Our crisis today is in reverse.

We find ourselves rich in goods, but ragged in spirit; reaching with magnificent precision for the moon, but falling into raucous discord on earth.

We are caught in war, wanting peace. We are torn by division, wanting unity. We see around us empty lives, wanting fulfillment. We see tasks that need doing, waiting for hands to do them.

To a crisis of the spirit, we need an answer of the spirit.

And to find that answer, we need only look within ourselves.

When we listen to "the better angels of our nature," we find that they celebrate the simple things, the basic things—such as goodness, decency, love, kindness.

Greatness comes in simple trappings.

The simple things are the ones most needed today if we are to surmount what divides us, and cement what unites us.

To lower our voices would be a simple thing.

In these difficult years, America has suffered from a fever of words; from inflated rhetoric that promises more than it can deliver; from angry rhetoric that fans discontents into hatreds; from bombastic rhetoric that postures instead of persuading.

We cannot learn from one another until we stop shouting at one another—until we speak quietly enough so that our words can be heard as well as our voices.

For its part, government will listen. We will strive to listen in new ways—to the voices of quiet anguish, the voices that speak without words, the voices of the heart—to the injured voices, the anxious voices, the voices that have despaired of being heard.

Those who have been left out, we will try to bring in.

Those left behind, we will help to catch up.

For all of our people, we will set as our goal the decent order that makes progress possible and our lives secure.

As we reach toward our hopes, our task is to build on what has gone before—not turning away from the old, but turning toward the new.

In this past third of a century, government has passed more laws, spent more money, initiated more programs, than in all our previous history.

In pursuing our goals of full employment, better housing, excellence in education; in rebuilding our cities and improving our rural areas; in protecting our environment and enhancing the quality of life—in all these and more, we will and must press urgently forward.

We shall plan now for the day when our wealth can be transferred from the destruction of war abroad to the urgent needs of our people at home.

The American dream does not come to those who fall asleep.

But we are approaching the limits of what government alone can do.

Our greatest need now is to reach beyond government, to enlist the legions of the concerned and the committed.

What has to be done, has to be done by government and people together or it will not be done at all. The lesson of past agony is that without the people we can do nothing—with the people we can do everything.

To match the magnitude of our tasks, we need the energies of our people—enlisted not only in grand enterprises, but more importantly in those small, splendid efforts that make headlines in the neighborhood newspaper instead of the national journal.

With these, we can build a great cathedral of the spirit—each of us raising it one stone at a time, as he reaches out to his neighbor, helping, caring, doing.

I do not offer a life of uninspiring ease. I do not call for a life of grim sacrifice. I ask you to join in a high adventure—one as rich as humanity itself, and exciting as the times we live in.

The essence of freedom is that each of us shares in the shaping of his own destiny.

Until he has been part of a cause larger than himself, no man is truly whole.

The way to fulfillment is in the use of our talents. We achieve nobility in the spirit that inspires that use.

As we measure what can be done, we shall promise only what we know we can produce; but as we chart our goals, we shall be lifted by our dreams.

No man can be fully free while his neighbor is not. To go forward at all is to go forward together.

This means black and white together, as one nation, not two. The laws have caught up with our conscience. What remains is to give life to what is in the law: to insure at last that as all are born equal in dignity before God, all are born equal in dignity before man.

As we learn to go forward together at home, let us also seek to go forward together with all mankind.

Let us take as our goal: where peace is unknown, make it welcome; where peace is fragile, make it strong; where peace is temporary, make it permanent.

After a period of confrontation, we are entering an era of negotiation.

Let all nations know that during this administration our lines of communication will be open.

We seek an open world—open to ideas, open to the exchange of goods and people—a world in which no people, great or small, will live in angry isolation.

We cannot expect to make everyone our friend, but we can try to make no one our enemy.

Those who would be our adversaries, we invite to a peaceful competition—not in conquering territory or extending dominion, but in enriching the life of man.

As we explore the reaches of space, let us go to the new worlds together—not as new worlds to be conquered, but as a new adventure to be shared.

With those who are willing to join, let us cooperate to reduce the burden of arms, to strengthen the structure of peace, to lift up the poor and the hungry.

But to all those who would be tempted by weakness, let us leave no doubt that we will be as strong as we need to be for as long as we need to be.

Over the past twenty years, since I first came to this Capital as a freshman congressman, I have visited most of the nations of the world. I have come to know the leaders of the world, and the great forces, the hatreds, the fears that divide the world.

I know that peace does not come through wishing for it—that there is no substitute for days and even years of patient and prolonged diplomacy.

I also know the people of the world.

I have seen the hunger of a homeless child, the pain of a man wounded in battle, the grief of a mother who has lost her son. I know these have no ideology, no race.

I know America. I know the heart of America is good.

I speak from my own heart, and the heart of my country, the deep concern we have for those who suffer, and those who sorrow.

I have taken an oath today in the presence of God and my countrymen to uphold and defend the Constitution of the United States. To that oath I now add this sacred commitment: I shall consecrate my Office, my energies, and all the wisdom I can summon to the cause of peace among nations.

Let this message be heard by strong and weak alike:

The peace we seek—the peace we seek to win—is not victory over any other people, but the peace that comes "with healing in its wings"; with compassion for those who have suffered; with understanding for those who have opposed us; with the opportunity for all the peoples of this earth to choose their own destiny.

Only a few short weeks ago we shared the glory of man's first sight of the world as God sees it, as a single sphere reflecting light in the darkness.

As Apollo astronauts flew over the moon's gray surface on Christmas Eve, they spoke to us of the beauty of earth—and in that voice so clear across the lunar distance, we heard them invoke God's blessing on its goodness.

In that moment, their view from the moon moved poet Archibald MacLeish to write: "To see the earth as it truly is, small and blue and beautiful in that eternal silence where it floats, is to see ourselves as riders on the earth together, brothers on that bright loveliness in the eternal cold—brothers who know now they are truly brothers."

In that moment of surpassing technological triumph, men turned their thoughts toward home and humanity—seeing in that far perspective that man's destiny on earth is not divisible; telling us that however far we reach into the cosmos, our destiny lies not in the stars but on earth itself, in our own hands, in our own hearts.

We have endured a long night of the American spirit. But as our eyes catch the dimness of the first rays of dawn, let us not curse the remaining dark. Let us gather the light.

Our destiny offers not the cup of despair, but the chalice of opportunity. So let us seize it not in fear, but in gladness—and "riders on the earth together," let us go forward, firm in our faith, steadfast in our purpose, cautious of the dangers; but sustained by our confidence in the will of God and the promise of man.

The Vice President Is Sworn In

In the slightly hunched stance of a big man who is used to dealing with people not as tall as he, Spiro Theodore Agnew placed his left hand on his daughter's open Bible and raised his right, palm open. He thus began a ceremony whose traditions are actually older—by nine days—than those of the presidential swearing-in. John Adams, the first Vice President, reached the temporary capital at New York a few days before Washington, and since the Senate was already in session and his job was to preside there, he took up his responsibilities as soon as arrangements were made. On April 21 he arrived in the Senate chamber, where John Langdon of New Hampshire, president pro tempore, gave the official greeting: "Sir, I have it in charge from the Senate to introduce you to the chair of this house and also to congratulate you on your appointment to the office of Vice President of the United States of America." Adams replied briefly, praising the assembled senators, and the ceremony, such as it was, was over. The first version of the pledge that, 180 years later, Vice President Agnew was to repeat, his hand on the Bible, was not made by Adams for several weeks. There was no oath for him to take; none but that for a President was specified in the Constitution, and it was not

until June 1 that oaths for other federal officers were provided. The wording of the Vice President's oath, included in the first law Washington signed, was the same as that for senators; it still is, although the oath has since been expanded.

The vice-presidential swearing-in has remained a brief prologue to the dramatic assumption of executive duties by a new President. In fact, until John Nance Garner was inaugurated for a second term under Franklin Roosevelt, the second man's oath-taking was normally held in the Senate, seen by few Americans—an event apart from the main business of the day. Garner, however,

made his pledge in 1937 on the stand before the Capitol, and succeeding Vice Presidents have done the same. Yet it is still a lesser moment, with a certain relaxedness about its form: in 1969 Senate Minority Leader Everett M. Dirksen administered the oath; in the past a variety of officers performed that function—retiring Vice Presidents, House Speakers, Senate presidents pro tem, an associate justice, a U.S. district attorney. Franklin Pierce's next-in-line, William R. D. King of Alabama, was in Cuba on Inauguration Day, trying vainly to recover from tuberculosis, and he was sworn in by a U.S. consul, though it took a special law to make it possible. King could not stand unaided, and he died only six weeks later.

A few other vice-presidential inaugurations were out of the ordinary. Andrew Johnson, recuperating from an illness in 1865, asked to be excused from the ceremonies, but Lincoln insisted he attend, and he did. In order to fight off nausea he drank some brandy (though he was not much of a drinker) and proceeded to play the most celebrated drunk scene in American politics, with an undignified harangue in the Senate about the dignity of the common man. It embarrassed everybody, including Johnson; he couldn't remember his words the next day. And in 1925 Vice President Charles G. Dawes stole the headlines from Calvin Coolidge by using the occasion of his swearing-in to lecture the Senate sternly on reform of its rules and procedures.

But most second men have by Inauguration Day accepted the restrictions that come with the job and have been careful to be relatively inconspicuous. Like Spiro Agnew, after the oath is taken the Vice President usually retires to the background, making his first address short and self-deprecating—mainly an appeal for the patience of the Senate toward the manner in which he will oversee its debate.

Left to right: President Johnson, Mrs. Everett M. Dirksen, President-elect Nixon, Senator Dirksen, Senate Minority Secretary J. Mark Trice, and Vice President Agnew.

A Gallery of Vice Presidents

Overshadowed by Washington, Adams saw his office as "the most insignificant that ever . . . man contrived." Gave senators long-winded explanations of his tie-breaking votes and lectured them on manners, morality, constitutional law. One of eight V.P.'s later elected President.

JOHN ADAMS
1789–97, Massachusetts

Ardent Revolutionist but inept troop commander; first governor of New York. As first V.P. elected under the Twelfth Amendment, he was the original ticket-balancer—for Jefferson, then for Madison. First V.P. to die in office. Uncle of DeWitt Clinton, projector of Erie Canal.

GEORGE CLINTON
1805–12, New York

The great southern parliamentarian served under both J. Q. Adams and Jackson. Broke with the latter over nullification and became the only V.P. to resign. In 43-year career, also served as senator, Secretary of War and of State. His prophetic last words (in March, 1850) were: "The South, the poor South."

JOHN CALDWELL CALHOUN
1825–32, South Carolina

Like John Adams under George Washington, Jefferson had little power in Adams' government. He was unable to block the Alien and Sedition acts or Jay's treaty with England, both of which he abhorred. But he wrote a *Manual of Parliamentary Practice*, which is the foundation of today's Senate procedures.

THOMAS JEFFERSON
1797–1801, Virginia

He served as Madison's second running mate and yet left no monument but "gerrymander," a word attached by one critic to a bill signed by Gerry as governor of Massachusetts to redistrict the state and assure a Republican majority in the legislature. He also died while still in office.

ELBRIDGE GERRY
1813–14, Massachusetts

A tavernkeeper's son, shrewd "Little Van" joined Jackson's Cabinet, won Old Hickory's confidence, then second place in the General's second term, finally designation as heir apparent. Third man elected to White House from the Vice Presidency. Early member of Tammany.

MARTIN VAN BUREN
1833–37, New York

Princeton grad (at 16), Revolutionary hero, brilliant New York lawyer. Fine Vice President, but ruined politically by his "murder" of Hamilton in duel. Later tried, but acquitted, of treasonous plot. At 78 this lifelong Don Juan, grandson of Jonathan Edwards, was sued for a divorce on the grounds of infidelity.

AARON BURR
1801–5, New York

A distinguished governor of New York in War of 1812, "the farmer's boy" was an undistinguished V.P. during both of Monroe's terms. Financial troubles, illness, and the bottle kept him away from Washington most of the time and destroyed brilliant promise of his early years.

DANIEL D. TOMPKINS
1817–25, New York

Hero of War of 1812, in which he allegedly slew Tecumseh. (His slogan as Van Buren's running mate: "Rumpsey, Dumpsey, Colonel Johnson killed Tecumseh.") First western V.P.; first elected by Senate (failed of electoral majority); first of three Vice Presidents named Johnson.

RICHARD MENTOR JOHNSON
1837–41, Kentucky

A states' rights man; hardly a Whig, but political needs put him on the 1840 ticket with "Tippecanoe" Harrison. As first V.P. to succeed a deceased President, he was called His Accidency. Married an heiress while in White House but died poor in 1862, having sided with South.

JOHN TYLER
1841, Virginia

An 1856 "convert" from Democratic party, Hamlin balanced the Lincoln ticket geographically, but his swarthy complexion gave rise to opposition charge that he was part Negro. He was a forthright advocate of emancipation. In the Senate after the war he joined the Radical Reconstruction faction.

HANNIBAL HAMLIN
1861-65, Maine

Henchman of Conkling political machine in New York. As collector of Port of New York, fired by President Hayes for abuse of office. Two years later elected V.P. with the doomed Garfield. A better fisherman than Chief Executive, but did get civil service reform legislation passed.

CHESTER ALAN ARTHUR
1881, New York

A Philadelphia lawyer and a very sociable ambassador to Russia, Dallas as Polk's V.P. was honest, competent, dignified. After his term in Washington he spent five years as Ambassador to Court of St. James. Texas city commemorates his name.

GEORGE MIFFLIN DALLAS
1845-49, Pennsylvania

A self-educated tailor, Johnson by 1853 had sewed up Tennessee politically and was elected governor. Never lost his feeling for the common man or against highborn. Succeeding the assassinated Lincoln, he fought Congress bitterly over Reconstruction; was impeached in 1868, acquitted by one vote.

ANDREW JOHNSON
1865, Tennessee

Born in Ohio, raised in Indiana; became political pro. U.S. senator from 1863 to '69, he was kingpin of Andrew Johnson's defense during impeachment trial. First Democratic governor elected (1872) in North after Civil War. Vice President with Cleveland in 1885 at age 65, died nine months later.

THOMAS ANDREWS HENDRICKS
1885, Indiana

First Vice President (and first President) born in nineteenth century. Like Tyler, he was nominated because of political expediency and succeeded to Presidency when his Chief died. Served out Zachary Taylor's term moderately well; authorized Commodore Perry's expedition to Japan.

MILLARD FILLMORE
1849-50, New York

Grant's first Vice President, an ambitious local politician from South Bend, Ind., whither his family migrated when he was a boy. He joined anything that might produce one or more votes, including, briefly, the Know-Nothings in 1855. Involvement in bribery finished him politically.

SCHUYLER COLFAX
1869-73, Indiana

Turned down chance to be Garfield's running mate. Among best V.P.'s and probably the richest. New York merchant prince during Civil War; in 1863 entered banking, rivaled J. P. Morgan. Ambassador to France, then Benjamin Harrison's V.P. Governor of New York when past 70.

LEVI PARSONS MORTON
1889-93, New York

This well-educated son of a Tarheel planter moved to Alabama, became one of its first U.S. senators. Elected with Franklin Pierce, King, who had gone to Cuba to cure his tuberculosis, was sworn in there by special act of Congress, but he died only a day after returning home.

WILLIAM RUFUS DEVANE KING
1853, Alabama

Born Jeremiah Colbaith in 1812; changed name to Henry Wilson for unknown reasons when he reached 21. Rose from shoemaker to factory owner, and was an early champion of the eight-hour day. Worked sixteen himself as ardent Lincoln man in Senate; wrote a history of the South. He died in office.

HENRY WILSON
1873-75, Massachusetts

Competent, affable, unsensational; Cleveland's second Vice President. Ran as V.P. candidate again in 1900 (with Bryan); failed against rough-riding opposition of T. Roosevelt. Grandsire of the 1952, 1956 Democratic candidate.

ADLAI EWING STEVENSON
1893-97, Illinois

One of ablest V.P.'s and the youngest, he came to office at 36 in tandem with Buchanan. He had pleaded for preservation of the Union, but in 1860 helped split it by running as southerners' presidential nominee. Joined the Confederacy, rose to be a major general and Jefferson Davis' Secretary of War.

JOHN CABELL BRECKINRIDGE
1857-61, Kentucky

"Who is Wheeler?" Rutherford B. Hayes inquired in 1876. Hayes found out shortly: despite lack of color, Vice President Wheeler was utterly honest, a loyal worker, a staunch supporter of civil service reform. Went home to Malone, N.Y., in 1881, relieved not to have become President himself.

WILLIAM ALMON WHEELER
1877-81, New York

His sound-money views made the wealthy Hobart a good running mate for McKinley. "An honest dollar . . . ," he said, "cannot be coined out of 53 cents of silver plus a legislative fiat." Fine president of Senate, though he cast tie-breaking vote against freedom for the Filipinos. Died in office at age 55.

GARRET AUGUSTUS HOBART
1897-99, New Jersey

Spent only five days presiding (badly) over Senate until adjournment. In September McKinley's death made T.R. at 42 our youngest President. "It is a dreadful thing to come into the Presidency this way," he said, "but it would be [far worse] to be morbid about it." He wasn't.

THEODORE ROOSEVELT
1901, New York

An immensely successful lawyer and financier, purchasing agent for the A.E.F. in 1918. Startling contrast with Coolidge: for every word Cal didn't say, Dawes said hundreds, salting them with favorite expressions like "Hell and Maria." As Hoover's ambassador, pleasantly surprised the Court of St. James.

CHARLES GATES DAWES
1925–29, Illinois

Born in a log cabin, Majority Leader of Senate under F.D.R., elected Veep (as he was affectionately called) at 71 under Truman. Famed as storyteller, *e.g.*, about a man's two sons: "One went to sea, the other was elected Vice President; he never heard of either of them again."

ALBEN WILLIAM BARKLEY
1949–53, Kentucky

An Ohio farmer's son, transplanted to Indiana, where he built a formidable political machine. Overshadowed by Teddy, Fairbanks got revenge in 1912 by helping to crush Roosevelt's drive for G.O.P. nomination. Four years later ran with Hughes against Wilson. Alaska's second city was named for him.

CHARLES WARREN FAIRBANKS
1905–9, Indiana

Part Kaw Indian; as a boy he rode bareback and hunted buffalo. Fresh from law studies, became reform hero as prosecuting attorney in dry Kansas, closing scores of saloons. Veteran representative and senator; as Vice President, substantially ignored by Hoover, who did not admire him.

CHARLES CURTIS
1929–33, Kansas

Lawyer and politician, foe of Alger Hiss, Vice President at mere 40. Eisenhower gave him unprecedentedly large role in Cabinet and security affairs. Made nine good-will trips abroad. Debated Khrushchev in Russia, Kennedy on television, lost the 1960 election by a whisker. Won on next try in 1968.

RICHARD MILHOUS NIXON
1953–61, California

"Sunny Jim," the pride of Utica, was a Throttlebottom but a first-rate presiding officer; he'd been in the House 20 years and trained under one of the best: Speaker Tom Reed. Ran again with Taft in 1912 but didn't live to see defeat: he died less than one week before election day.

JAMES SCHOOLCRAFT SHERMAN
1909–12, New York

A Texas politician of the old brand, "Cactus Jack" served 30 years in Congress, becoming Speaker in 1931. Agreed to run with F.D.R. to keep 1932 convention from deadlock. Worked closely with Roosevelt at first, but cool to New Deal after 1936. Died just short of his 99th birthday in 1967.

JOHN NANCE GARNER
1933–41, Texas

Grandson of a Confederate soldier; grew up in Johnson City, Texas; served in Congress 24 years. Protégé of F.D.R.; skillful, popular, folksy Senate leader. Like Mr. Nixon, given busy role by his Chief. When sworn in on plane at Dallas airport, at 55, became first southern President since Reconstruction era.

LYNDON BAINES JOHNSON
1961–63, Texas

First V.P. since Calhoun to be re-elected. He refused to "usurp" the stricken Wilson's place in 1919; when a hoaxer told him the President had died, he almost collapsed himself. His wry humor ("What this country needs is a really good five-cent cigar") helped make him a popular V.P.

THOMAS RILEY MARSHALL
1913–21, Indiana

Scion of distinguished Iowa farmer-editors, he became an authority on corn. New Deal Secretary of Agriculture, 1933–40; thereafter an active V.P., example of the envoy-at-large type. Ousted from Truman Cabinet for criticizing foreign policy; ran independently for President in 1948. Died in 1965.

HENRY AGARD WALLACE
1941–45, Iowa

South Dakota druggist's son, entered national politics in 1948; from then to 1964 served as Minnesota senator. Able, talkative, was characterized by Johnson as unlike "the other liberals. He wanted to get the job done." Elected Vice President in 1964. Democratic candidate for President in 1968.

HUBERT HORATIO HUMPHREY
1965–69, Minnesota

"Coolidge—my God!" said Henry Cabot Lodge when "Silent Cal" was mentioned for V.P. in 1916. Four years later, his reputation undeservedly enhanced by his handling of a Boston police strike, Gov. Coolidge reached that high place and, when Warren G. Harding died suddenly, a higher place still.

CALVIN COOLIDGE
1921–23, Massachusetts

Farmer, captain in the A.E.F., and unsuccessful haberdasher, he entered Missouri politics under Boss Pendergast, as a minor judge. Seeking promotion, was told by Pendergast, "The best I can do right now, Harry, is a U.S. senatorship." But he made a fine senator. He was Vice President for exactly 83 days.

HARRY S. TRUMAN
1945, Missouri

A governor whose rise was little short of meteoric; not well known outside Maryland before his effective handling of civil disorders in April, 1968, "Ted" Agnew was Vice President-elect that November. Elected executive of Baltimore County in 1962 and Governor of Maryland in 1966; selected by Mr. Nixon, who wanted a Vice President who had urban-government experience and border-state appeal.

SPIRO THEODORE AGNEW
1969–   , Maryland

Vice President Fillmore (top) chairs the Senate during debate on the 1850 Compromise.

Duties of the Vice President

*O*f all the comments, unflattering and otherwise, that Vice Presidents have made about their office, the one that capsulized the job best—at least until World War II—was delivered by the first incumbent. "I am possessed of two separate powers," said John Adams, "the one *in esse* and the other *in posse*. I am Vice President. In this I am nothing, but I may be everything. . . ."

The day-to-day constitutional duties of the Vice President—the *esse* to which Adams referred—were limited to presiding over the Senate and, when necessary, breaking ties with a casting vote. This job, of course, could involve a good deal of real power. As Harry Truman phrased it, "The opportunities afforded by the Vice Presidency, particularly the Presidency of the Senate, do not come—they are there to be seized. . . ." Adams provided a good example. Feeling that the office was beneath his talents and experience anyway, he set about making the most of it. He often delivered speeches from the chair, took part in debate, scolded the Senate for its behavior, and generally made his presence felt in support of the administration. Because the Senate was for a while very small and often evenly divided, he had the opportunity to use his casting vote twenty-nine times—still a record. Thomas Jefferson, though not as aggressive a presiding officer, added to the spirit of vice-presidential control of debate by writing a book on parliamentary practice that remains the basis for Senate procedure. Aaron Burr, who succeeded him, also kept a tight rein on the Senate, calling the members to order for trading insults, for wandering around during debate, and for not hewing to the point when speaking. But after Burr the power of the Vice President declined.

The Twelfth Amendment, requiring electors to specify their choices for President and Vice President—rather than vote for two men as President—made a cautious choice of second man less necessary than it had been: there was now no chance that a man intended for the Vice Presidency would be elected President. The 66-year-old George Clinton followed the 49-year-old Burr in the chair. Clinton was not in good health, he was not especially faithful to his duties, and when he did preside the Senate wished he hadn't. "Mr. Clinton," wrote John Quincy Adams, "is totally ignorant of all the most common forms of proceeding in Senate. . . . His judgement is neither quick nor strong. . . . As the only duty of a Vice President . . . is to preside in Senate, it ought to be considered what his qualifications for that office are at his election. In this respect

a worse choice than Mr. Clinton could scarcely have been made." Clinton died in his second term and was followed by another superannuated patriot, Elbridge Gerry, who was nearly sixty-nine ("a respectable old man, but weak and worn out," commented the French minister); Gerry died less than two years later. His successor, Daniel D. Tompkins, was a younger man, but personal problems distracted him from his duties during the eight years he was Monroe's next-in-line.

Until Tompkins' second term, Senate committees had normally been appointed by a Senate vote, but in Tompkins' absence the upper house was chaired by the graceful and skilled John Gaillard of South Carolina, and in 1823 the Senate turned over the responsibility for making committee appointments to "the presiding officer of this House." So when the brilliant John Calhoun picked up the gavel as John Quincy Adams' Vice President, he had an opportunity not only to reassert former powers for his office but also to solidify a new and meaningful duty. He frittered the chances away. He employed the appointing power in his fight against Adams and in his own drive for the Presidency; he loaded committees with anti-administration men, and the Senate was so outraged at being used in this fashion that it restored the old balloting system. Seldom in the subsequent history of the Senate has the Vice President been allowed to name committees. Calhoun further diminished the duties of his office by his attitude toward the conduct of debate in the Senate. Wishing to ingratiate himself with its members, viewing the Senate as the meeting place for ambassadors from sovereign and independent republics—ambassadors who had not personally elected him to preside over them—he refused to call speakers to order for personal attacks or for failing to stick to the question being debated. President Adams was the target of considerable verbal acid in the Senate, and he recalled later, with pardonable exaggeration, that Calhoun permitted "John Randolph, . . . day after day, in speeches of ten hours long, to drink himself drunk with bottled porter, and in raving balderdash . . . , to revile the absent and the present, the living and the dead. . . ." To criticism of his laxness, Calhoun replied that he had "an appellate power only," which could not be activated until the offending senator was called to order by one of his peers. Exasperated, the Senate finally changed the rules so that the Chair was impelled to call members to order on his own initiative —with, however, a new restriction: any such call to order could be overruled by the Senate.

Succeeding Vice Presidents were chary of calling to

order, and the Senate itself grew increasingly protective of its rights in regard to the Vice President. A member once pointedly reminded Vice President James S. Sherman that "the Senate is a *self-governing* body," and Vice President Thomas R. Marshall conceded that he was "merely nominally presiding" over the upper chamber.

A good deal of the limitation on vice-presidential duties in practice stems from the peculiar position of the office—someplace between the executive and legislative branches of the government, sometimes watched suspiciously by both, and having responsibilities to both. The power wielded and the duties performed by a given individual in the office have mainly depended on two factors. If he should be a trusted ally of the President, he might be employed on the Hill to push administration measures or be given special jobs to do. If he should be a former legislator, particularly a former senator, he might be treated as a member-emeritus of The Club and his opinions carry weight both on the Hill and at the White House. If, as has often happened, he represented a faction opposed to the administration, he might also have negative powers, acting as a rallying point for presidential enemies and helping to block legislation being pushed by the executive.

In general, however, it has been only in the last few decades that, with the exception of the minor duty of presiding over the Senate and considerable social responsibilities as a Washington dinnertime representative of the President, the Vice President has had anything of importance to perform unless the President gave it to him. In 1846 the second officer was made a statutory member of the Board of Regents of the Smithsonian Institution, but as Tom Marshall remarked, "There, if anywhere, he has an opportunity to compare his fossilized life with the fossils of all ages."

The office was famous as a do-nothing post; it was the butt of much humor. And partly because of that it has changed since Marshall's day. This coincided with the increase in the responsibilities of the executive branch. As long ago as the Civil War—when the executive for a while became the focus of American government—President Lincoln brought Hannibal Hamlin into regular participation in the administration. Marshall (under protest, feeling that it compromised his relationship with the legislature) presided over the Cabinet at Wilson's behest when the President went to Europe in 1918. The popular Calvin Coolidge sat in Harding's Cabinet, saying little but learning a lot. On the grounds that such a practice should not be per-

mitted to become routine because it might tie a President's hands in the future, the officious Charles G. Dawes publicly refused to participate in the meetings of Coolidge's Cabinet—before Coolidge had offered him the chance. But every Vice President since then has joined those sessions, and beginning with Richard Nixon, all have presided over the Cabinet whenever the President was absent.

The deaths in office of eight Presidents, and the close calls in several other cases, have gradually impressed on the American consciousness the need to prepare the next-in-line for some of the problems he might have to face in an emergency. That is one reason he now sits with the Cabinet. Harry Truman, who had not even heard of the atomic bomb when Franklin Roosevelt died, took the trend toward preparation a step farther and convinced Congress to make the Vice President a member, by law, of the National Security Council. The second officer is now also the statutory chairman of the National Space Council. Since the days of Jack Garner, the Vice President has often served as a special diplomatic representative. Franklin Roosevelt made Henry Wallace, his second Vice President, chairman of various committees in the executive branch, and subsequent Presidents have followed this lead: Vice President Agnew, among other responsibilities, heads the new Office of Intergovernmental Relations.

"In this I am nothing . . ." is a statement John Adams would not make today as Vice President. ". . . but I may be everything." Eight times the Vice President has been required to perform the second duty given his office by the Constitution—that of assuming executive leadership of the nation when the elected President is no longer able to exercise it. But if the Founding Fathers gave the second office a short straw in terms of daily duties, they left it in utter perplexity in terms of this most crucial responsibility.

"In Case of the Removal of the President from Office," said the clause in Article II, Section 1, "or of his Death, Resignation, or Inability to discharge the Powers and Duties of the said Office, the Same shall devolve on the Vice President. . . ." Scholars and politicos have probed those words ever since, and have argued vigorously over what they mean. "The Same shall devolve on the Vice President. . . ." The same what? "The Office?" Or "the Powers and Duties of the said Office?" Was the Vice President, in short, to become President, or only Acting President? The clause lumped together removal, death, resignation, and inability as cases in which the Vice President was to assume whatever it was he was to assume. So the status he had when a President died, he also had in every other case in which he was supposed to take on executive responsibility. Thus it was that when William Henry Harrison fell ill in the first month of his term, and the fledgling administration ground to a halt, his Cabinet decided not to call in John Tyler to fulfill executive responsibilities while Harrison lived; evidently it was believed, particularly by Secretary of State Daniel Webster, that once Tyler took over it would be for the rest of the four-year term, not just until Harrison got well. Most of the Congress, as well as the Cabinet, approved when Tyler assumed the *office* of President on Harrison's death, although at least one legislator pointed out the dangers of setting such a precedent. One of the most remarkable aspects of this event was the fact that the lawmakers apparently ignored an applicable clause in the Twelfth Amendment: there it was stated that in a contested election, if the House of Representatives had not chosen a President by Inauguration Day, "then the Vice Pres-

August 3, 1923: Harding has died, and before dawn Calvin Coolidge is sworn in as the 30th President by his father, in the sitting room of the Coolidges' Vermont home.

ident *shall act as President, as in the case of the death or other constitutional disability of the President.*" [Italics supplied.] It has proven valuable that on the death of a President the next-in-line assumes a position in the government that is diminished not at all, in a legal sense, from that of an elected Chief Executive. But Tyler's precedent was to hamstring the government and place the Vice President in an embarrassing position in every situation where a President became too ill to serve—Garfield's and Wilson's cases being the most conspicuous examples; a contributing factor, of course, was the Constitution's failure to spell out, as one of its authors had commented, "What is the extent of the term 'disability' & who is to be the judge of it? . . ." Tom Marshall was offered all kinds of support for any move he might decide to make while Wilson lay desperately ill. He would not act, remarking, "I am not going to seize the place, and then have Wilson recovered, come around and say, 'Get off, you usurper.'"

President Eisenhower, whose contributions to the office of Vice President were the most important in our history, failed to get Congress to pass an amendment clarifying the inability question and came up with a makeshift solution in the form of a letter of understanding to Vice President Nixon in which the procedures Nixon was to follow in case of a disabling presidential illness were spelled out. Presidents Kennedy and Johnson did the same with their Vice Presidents, and finally, during Johnson's administration, the entire succession clause in the Constitution was amended. Now on a President's death the Vice President becomes President; but in serious presidential illnesses he becomes Acting President. Either the President, if he is able, or, if not, the Vice President and a majority of the Cabinet or a majority of "such other body as Congress may by law provide" can declare presidential incapacity to serve. The President can pick up the reins again simply by declaring he is ready to, unless the Vice President and the specified advisory body disagree. In that case Congress must meet and decide within twenty-one days who is right, and if it doesn't make a formal decision the President automatically takes over again. One can read a few hair-raising possibilities into this system, but it is a vast improvement over what prevailed for more than 175 years.

So the post into which Spiro Theodore Agnew was inaugurated on January 20, 1969, is better defined, is larger, and has more responsibilities than ever before, though it remains, as the Vice President's predecessor put it, an "awkward office."

Inaugural Parades
in History

Pennsylvania Avenue, the nation's parade route: looking toward the Capitol in 1837.

Except for the presidential oath of office, the parade probably has been the one ceremony among all the customary Inauguration Day proceedings that is most honored by time. Generations of custom have almost frozen its form and its content: the route is carefully defined, the military bands are well-rehearsed, the states have planned their floats with great ingenuity and executed them with artistry. Nevertheless, the long march-by often appears to take on some spontaneous-appearing quality that provides a traditional event with at least some suggestion of unpredictability. Small boys dash from the crowd into the ranks, disrupting step and sometimes key. Horses behave improperly. The music—except when it comes abreast—provides only a distant background to the clamor of cheering, conversation, and the shrill whistles of drum major-

ettes. No one really cares; this is a day when one has no purpose except to celebrate and enjoy. No one is reviewing the military units as they go by except the President who has just been inaugurated—and at the moment he is usually so excited that he would probably excuse a military unit for marching backwards.

In the early days the trappings were extremely casual. George Washington was escorted from his quarters in New York to Federal Hall on Wall Street by a "joint committee of Congress" of eight men, followed by various officials—apparently in an informal stroll—although these politicians were followed in the line of march by several units of the Army of the very, very young United States, while a group of leading citizens brought up the rear.

Thomas Jefferson, the great democrat, went to the

Frank Leslie's Illustrated Newspaper, MARCH 19, 1881

The parade celebrating James Garfield's 1881 inauguration, as seen from the Capitol.

Because March 4 was a Sunday in 1877, Rutherford B. Hayes was sworn in privately at the White House Saturday night and inaugurated publicly on Monday. That night a huge torchlight parade marched up Pennsylvania Avenue to the White House, while fireworks banged and flashed.

84

Capitol in characteristic manner, accompanied at his first inauguration by a couple of his Cabinet officers, some members of Congress, and a number of citizens, although there was a company of Maryland artillery to give the semblance of a parade.

With the inauguration of James Madison in 1809 the parade adopted its military formality. The times may have had something to do with this, for tensions among the United States, England, and France were high and the War of 1812 was near. Cavalry escorted Madison to the Capitol, guns boomed as he took the oath, and militia lined his path as he walked from the Capitol to his carriage after he had taken the oath. There was no threat of war when James Monroe and John Quincy Adams were sworn in, but the military flourish remained in the parades.

Ironically, it was a military man, the first general since Washington, who broke the developing precedent of a military parade. Andrew Jackson did not want a parade, vetoed the plans for one, and walked along the sidewalk with his friends while the old guard scoffed at his lack of form. Not all who watched the walk maintained their scorn, however. The grand simplicity of it struck Francis Scott Key as "Sublime!" and one Washington lady who once may have thought herself anti-Jackson said, "It is *true* greatness which needs not the aid of ornament and pomp. I think I shall like him vastly when I know him."

Today's reader will not fail to be struck by one aspect of these early parades that is the complete opposite of those of today. They all went *to* the Capitol, for their organizers saw them as ceremonial escorts for the President-elect on his way to take the oath of office. It would still be a long time before they started going the other way.

Martin Van Buren followed Jackson in 1837 and there was a parade again, though not an imposing one: a small unit of infantry and cavalry and a good many civilians. It took the supporters of William Henry "Old Tippecanoe" Harrison to show what an Inaugural Parade could be. Harrison had been elected over Van Buren in 1840 in a campaign of political ballyhoo, and the parade was cut out of the same pattern; it was filled with Tippecanoe clubs, log cabins, college-student groups, and, of course, military bands and militia units.

Harper's Weekly, MARCH 13, 1897

A new note was also added to the ceremonies at James Buchanan's inauguration in 1857: the parade was led by a huge float bearing a woman representing the goddess of liberty. Another float, a model of a warship, followed the President-elect's carriage.

The military emphasis in Lincoln's parades was functional; because the President's life was in danger he rode well protected and surrounded by soldiers bearing loaded weapons. The military aspect of Grant's two parades was made almost ridiculous by the addition to the line of march of virtually any group that came dressed in any uniform: firemen, Union veterans, and an assortment of members of men's clubs.

With the inauguration of Benjamin Harrison in 1889 the parade ceased to be an escort to the Capitol for the President-elect. Instead, after he was sworn in, Harrison had lunch at the White House and then went to a reviewing stand to watch the march-by, which not only included numerous military units, but such diverse elements as Buffalo Bill leading a cowboy contingent, a group of firemen, red-shirted and carrying red, white, and blue umbrellas, and a contingent carrying flaming torches. The parade was so long that darkness fell before it was over, and some units broke up without passing the reviewing stand.

Theodore Roosevelt, needless to say, did things with his usual flair. There were soldiers aplenty at his 1905 inaugural, but they were overshadowed by legions of whooping Indians, yodeling cowboys, and, of course, the exuberant Rough Riders, still popular seven years after their Cuban adventure in the Spanish-American War. Roosevelt enjoyed it all thoroughly, calling out from time to time from his reviewing stand to the passing paraders.

The automobile lessened the military nature of the Inaugural Parade, if only because a line of black convertibles traveling slowly between ranks of marching, uniformed men looks somewhat incongruous. And for an older generation, parades have never been the same since the passing of the horse, but younger Americans think it entirely natural to have everything mechanized. But whatever the complaints, they are small, and the Inaugural Parade is a pretty satisfactory spectacle. After all, it is meant to be no more than that, a time to relax and enjoy after the solemnity of the inauguration of the President.

A delegation of veterans of the Grand Army of the Republic came to Washington to take part in the parade at McKinley's second inaugural. But they were assigned to the tail end of the line and, piqued, refused to march at all.

The 1969
Inaugural Parade

In the reviewing stand, the President reaches over to squeeze Mrs. Eisenhower's hand.

A company of West Point cadets swings onto Fifteenth Street from Pennsylvania Avenue.

FORWARD TOGETHER

A float celebrating the thought "Up With People" passes before the Treasury Building.

Above, Governor and Mrs. Ronald Reagan of California acknowledge applause. Below, Miss Indian American XV —Thomasine Hill of Crow Agency, Montana—rides in the parade, one of hundreds of Indian Americans taking part.

Color guard representing Maryland passes the reviewing stand and dips its state flags.

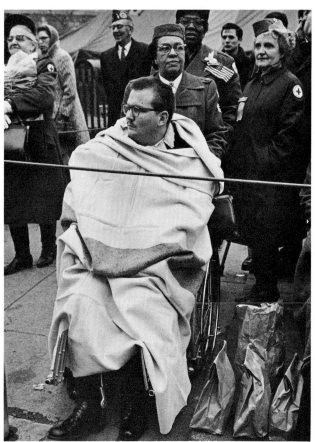

Above, while the President watched the parade from one side of Pennsylvania Avenue, some of his special guests—war veterans and Medal of Honor winners—observed it from a spot facing him. Below, the float of the State of Mississippi.

THE PEACEABLE KINGDOM

WASHINGTON

FORWARD TOGETHER · THE SKY'S THE LIMIT

The aircraft industry is featured on the State of Washington's float, at left. Below, Puerto Rico's float depicts in block letters the island's interests in tourism and commerce. The order of march, in terms of the states, was based on date of entry into the Union; the territories came after the states. So by the time the contingents from Washington—the forty-second state—and Puerto Rico reached the reviewing stand, darkness had fallen on the marchers.

The tradition of the Inaugural Ball has been remarkably various. Above is a ticket to the stylish (though a bit gloomy) party that followed Buchanan's inauguration.

Inaugural Balls of Yesterday

The first presidents took the oath of office and went about their business. Washington, inaugurated in New York, attended St. Paul's Church for services and returned to his home. At night there was a fireworks display from Fort George in New York Bay; Washington watched from the house of a friend and walked home through streets crowded with celebrants. John Adams had lunch as usual at his boardinghouse in Philadelphia. There was a ball that evening, but it was for the retiring President, Washington, and no one thought to invite Adams. The first Chief Executive to be inaugurated in Washington, Thomas Jefferson did not go to the White House after his swearing-in, returning instead to his boardinghouse, where he sat at the dinner table with the other boarders, in his customary chair near the foot of the table, far from the warming fire.

With James Madison the post-inaugural celebrations began to assume the formality of affairs of state. The primary force behind the festivities was Madison's popular wife, Dolley, who was, for all intents and purposes, the initial First Lady to actively interpret her role as that of official hostess of the United States.

Soon after the ceremonies at the Capitol, the Madisons returned to their home in Georgetown, where they received legions of callers at a formal reception and served them punch and cake. At seven o'clock in the evening, the first Inauguration Ball began at Long's Hotel. Thomas Jefferson arrived early, in high spirits at being a private citizen again. "You must tell me how to behave," he said to a friend, perhaps facetiously, "for it is more than forty years since I have been to a ball." Four hundred people were present, with the diplomatic corps, finely attired in their uniforms, adding to the colorful formality. On the whole, however, the ball was something of a rose in a thorn patch: Washington was still a skeleton of a city, with a few scattered buildings, many unsightly, its streets muddy and un-

Overleaf: Andrew Jackson's reception was a mob scene.

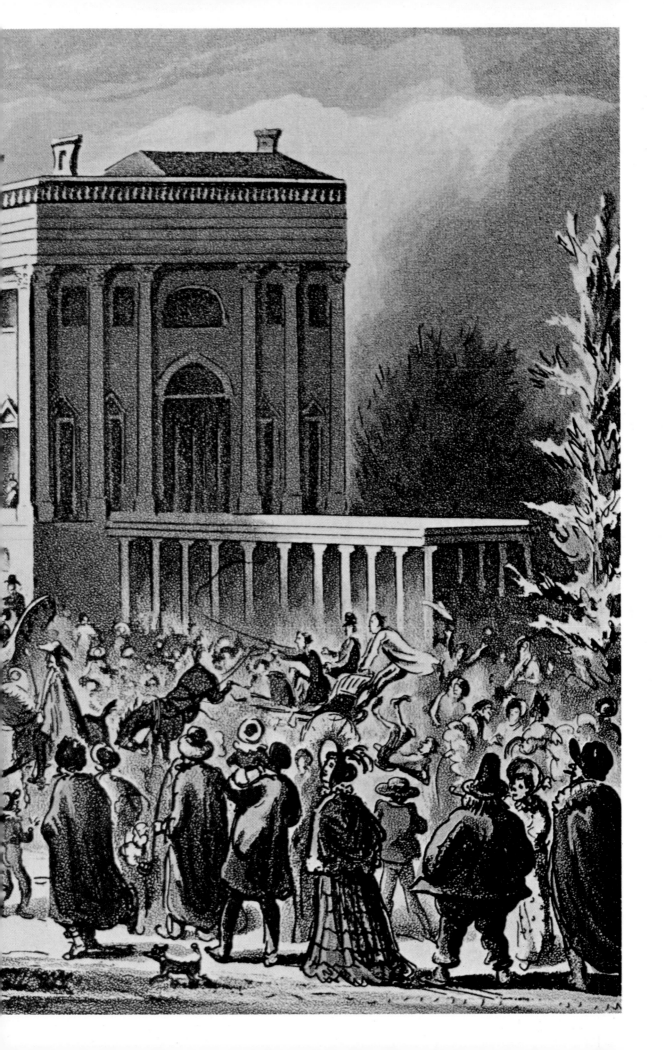

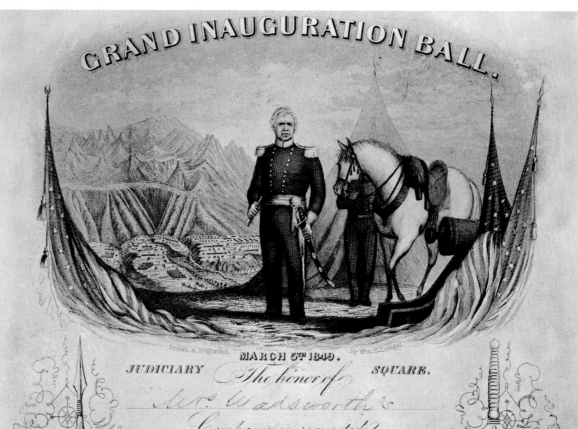

GRAND INAUGURATION BALL.

Drawn & Engraved   by Wm H Dougal

MARCH 5TH 1849.

JUDICIARY   *The honor of*   SQUARE.

Mrs Wadsworth

Company is requested

MANAGERS.

Hon. R. C. Winthrop, Speaker.
. W. P. Mangum, N. C.
. Hiram Belcher, Me.
. James Wilson, N. H.
. S. S. Phelps, Vt.
. Truman Smith, Ct.
. Albert C. Green, R. I.
. Geo. Ashmun, Mass.
. John Bell, Tenn.
. Hugh White, N. Y.
. Jacob W. Miller, N. J.
. F. A. Tallmadge, N. J.
. Reverdy Johnson, Md.
. Wm. B. Preston, Va.
. J. A. Pearce, Md.
. Robt. W. Johnson, Ark.
. William Upham, Vt.
. Caleb B. Smith, Ia.
. R. McClelland, Mich.
. M. C. Darling, Wis.
. D. M. Barringer, N. C.
. John G. Chapman, Md.
. James Dixon, Conn.
. A. H. Stephens, Geo.
. J. S. Gregory, N. J.
. Joseph Grinnell, Mass.
. W. Hunt, N. Y.
. C. S. Morehead, Ken.
. J. P. Gaines, Ken.
. J. Dixon Roman, Md.
. R. C. Schenck, Ohio.
. Thos Corwin, Ohio.
. J. R. Ingersoll, Pa.
. J. R. Underwood, Ky.
. Isaac E. Holmes, S. C.
. Thomas H. Benton, Mo.
. Robert Toombs, Geo.
. Thomas J. Rusk, Texas
. Hugh Barrow, Tenn.
. W. L. Dayton, N. J.
. P. W. Tompkins, Miss.
. Henry Johnson, La.
. Thos B. King, Ga.
. John Gayle, Ala.
. Abraham Lincoln, Ill.
. Wm. Thompson, Iowa.
. John L. Taylor, Ohio.
. E. C. Cabell, Fla.
. Green Adams, Ken.
. C. Butler, Penn.
. R. B. Cranston, R. I.
. B. S. Donnell, N. C.
. G. Duncan, Ken.
. M. P. Gentry, Tenn.
. J. G. Hampton, N. J.
. J. W. Houston, Del.
. J. S. Pendleton, Va.
. D. B. St. John, N. Y.
. A. Stewart, Penn.
. B. G. Thibodaux, La.
. J. B. Thompson, Ken.
. Thos. O. Edwards, Ohio.
. J. E. Brady, Penn.
. Aylett Buckner, Ken.

Major Gen. Winfield Scott.
Gen. George Gibson.
Adjt. Gen. Roger Jones .
Col. R. E. Lee .
Lieut. col. John Mc. Clelland .
Capt. W. Morris .
Gen. J. G. Totten .
Lieut. col. R. C. Buchanan .
Major J. D. Graham .
Col. J. E. Johnston .
Capt. John Lee .
Maj. Johns .
Com. Charles Morris .
. I. Warrington .
. C. W. Morgan .
Capt. French Forrest .
. L. M. Powell .
. J. S. Chauncey .
Lieut. Cad. Ringgold .
. Charles Turner .
. Chas. Steedman .
. C. Price .
. Marwell Woodhull .
. S. C. Barney .
Major James Edelin .
. P. G. Howle .
Henry Addison .
Hugh Caperton .
George C. Washington .   Geo. Town
O. M. Linthicum .
W. W. Seaton, Mayor .
Daniel Carroll of Duddington .
George W. P. Custis .
Joseph Gales .
R. C. Weightman .
Peter Force .
J. H. Mc. Blair .
B. O. Taylee .
E. Kingman .
Gov. S. Sprigg .
Walter Lenox .
Silas H. Hill .
Clement Hill .
Robert Farnham .
Gen. Walter Jones .
Lewis Johnson .
Wm. Cost Johnson .
W. W. Corcoran .
J. P. Haliday .
Clement March .
S. L. Governeur .
Robert S. Patterson .
John A. Linton .
J. B. H. Smith .
Robert H. Williamson .
Dewitt Kent .
Judge J. Bryan .
S. F. Franklin .
Dr. J. C. Hall .
Dr. Thomas Miller .
J. W. Moorhead .
F. D. Schenck .
J. Madison Cutts .
William Wilson .

J. Munroe Chubb
Augustus Jay
Dr. T. B. J. Frye .
P. H. Brooks .
A. B. Claxton .
F. Schroeder Jr .
Thomas W. Howard .
C. W. Blackwell .
Charles Maury .
W. F. Anderson .
Hudson Taylor .
W. A. Kennedy .
Francis Y. Naylor .
A. B. Clements .
J. L. Henshaw .
Richard Wallach .
Joseph H. Bradley .
W. H. Winter .
John A. Smith .
John F. Coyle .
W. A. Bradley .
Beverly Tucker .
John T. Towers .
Edward Simms .
George W. Riggs .
B. L. Jackson .
J. M. Carlisle .
C. E. Sherman .
Columbus Munroe .
P. R. Fendall .
Ignatius Mudd .
George S. Gideon .
Francis Mohun .
Frank Taylor .
Stanislaus Murray .
Thomas S. Smith .
Peter H. Hoce .
Dr. C. Boyle .
Thomas L. Thruston .
W. H. Gunnell .
Alexander Lee .
Marshall Brown .
George Watterston .
W. G. Mc. Donald .
William Gadsby .
James Adams .
Dr. N. Young .
Jonas B. Ellis .
W. J. Mc. Cormick .
Truxton Beale .
H. B. Sweeny .
A. W. Fletcher .
C. F. Lowrey .
John W. Martin .
H. W. Willard .
Lemuel J. Middleton .
Isaac Hall .
Andrew Coyle Jr .
R. M. Coombs .
Jonathan Prout .
John Carroll Brent .
Dr. J. M. Thomas .
Wm. B. Webb .
Geo. Harrington

PALO ALTO

ZACHARY TAYLOR

RESACA DE LA PALMA

MONTEREY

MILLARD FILLMORE

BUENA VISTA

paved. The foreigners present must have thought the setting odd for so grand and pompous a fete.

By the time of James Monroe's inauguration in 1817, the city was in worse, not better, shape; the British burning of 1814 had not yet been repaired. The contrast, then, between setting and celebration must have been even more startling; for Mrs. Monroe, a Francophile and admirer of courtly manners, was a more imposing, more formal woman than Mrs. Madison. Still, the reception at the Monroe's temporary home—the White House was still being rebuilt after its destruction at the hands of the British—and the ball at Davis' Hotel were pleasant affairs, without the sometimes offensive selectivity that made Mrs. Monroe's later social events sources of contention in the capital.

John Quincy Adams, a less sociable animal than his predecessors, nevertheless followed their precedents, greeting afternoon visitors and attending an evening ball. Adams had defeated Andrew Jackson, the leader in the popular vote, through what many bitterly claimed was a corrupt deal. That night Jackson gave his own banquet for his partisans, who wanted nothing to do with Adams.

Probably the most disastrous of all post-inaugural celebrations was the reception that followed Andrew Jackson's first swearing-in in 1829. Jackson's wife had died only recently, and so an official ball was eliminated from the schedule. But since Old Hickory was the people's President, the hero of the common man, he thought it appropriate to conduct open house at the Executive Mansion after his inauguration for the thousands of common men who had converged on Washington for the great event. The hungry mob descended on the White House, stepping with muddy boots onto damask-covered chairs, knocking over furniture and glassware to get at the barrels of orange punch, ice cream, and cake that had been provided. One southern visitor commented that "it would have done Mr. Wilberforce's [an English abolitionist] heart good to have seen a stout black wench eating jelley with a gold spoon in the President's House." Most alarming of all was the press of the crowd to shake President Jackson's hand. Exhausted, helpless, cornered, and almost suffocating, Jackson was unable to free himself. Finally a number of men forced their way through the people, formed a cordon around Old Hickory, and, locking arms, drove a flying wedge through the mob and out a back door. Jackson returned to his room at Gadsby's Tavern; meanwhile at the White House, the attendants began placing the food and barrels of punch on the lawn to draw the people from the mansion.

To accommodate the ever-enlarging demand for tickets to the Inaugural Ball, Martin Van Buren started the practice of having two balls, an expensively ticketed one (which he attended) at Carusi's and a cheaper one elsewhere. Though the practice was not well received— many of the guests at the lesser ball were offended—it continued anyway. William Henry Harrison expanded the number to three (all of which he visited), and Polk returned to two—a ten-dollar version and a five-dollar bargain.

Ironically, the Inaugural Ball generally regarded as the first truly successful one, appropriate to the dignity of the Presidency and to the meaningfulness of the event, was conducted by America's first bachelor President, James Buchanan, in 1857. Held in a specially built structure, 235 feet long and 77 feet wide, the ball was presided over by the President's competent official hostess, his niece, Harriet Lane. But if the preparations were expert and the grandeur appropriate, the atmosphere of Washington was heavy with illness and nervous anticipation. Dysentery had infected several political figures. Called the "National Hotel disease," it was believed to have been caused by the emigration of rats during a freeze from the walls of that hotel into the plumbing, where they contaminated the water supply. The hotel was the most popular in town among government people, and even Buchanan had been infected. But the mood of the country, divided as never before and approaching the brink of civil war, was the more serious damper on inaugural gaiety. The Russian minister, dancing with the wife of the French envoy, reminded her of the Comte de Salvardy's comment at a fete in Paris just before the Revolution of 1830: "We are dancing on a volcano."

In the even more somber atmosphere of 1861, President Lincoln held a post-inaugural reception and spent some of the afternoon at work. At the Union Ball held

At left is an invitation to the ball held in honor of Zachary Taylor and Vice President Millard Fillmore. The Spanish names woven into the design represent the Mexican War victories that had raised General Taylor to prominence.

in a new building in Judiciary Square at night, he shook hands from eight-thirty until ten-thirty, then led a grand march at eleven. Despite the efforts of the guests to enjoy themselves, the ball seemed strange and strained. The main reason was the general somberness of the time, but the atmosphere was also affected by the absence of southerners. True, not many of the guests were well disposed toward their seceding countrymen, but Washington society to a substantial extent had been the creation of southerners; and without the people who had given the city its social tone, everyone else tended to feel as though they were guests without hosts.

Ulysses S. Grant's two inaugurations were notable for discomforts suffered by ball goers. The 1869 ball was held in the north wing of the Treasury Building, and was open to anyone who paid the required ten dollars. As a result, the crush was extreme, and the organization minimal. Confusion in the cloakroom was so bad that many guests waited hours to reclaim their wraps, and some went home uncovered. The 1873 ball was held in a temporary building of flimsy construction, the weather was intensely cold, and no one had thought to provide heat. Most of the miserable guests—they paid twenty dollars that year—passed up a sumptuous "cold collation" and went home early.

Rutherford B. Hayes was denied an Inaugural Ball in 1877 because his election was in doubt until only three days before Inauguration Day. In 1881 President Garfield tried to compensate for its absence four years earlier by holding one of the most colorful Inaugural Balls, a brilliant affair held amid a profusion of roses at the new National Museum, while two bands played and an enormous buffet was served.

With the first inauguration of Grover Cleveland, the vast Pension Building in Washington became, for a time, the standard site of Inaugural Balls. Benjamin Harrison held his celebration there in 1889, as did Cleveland once more when he returned to the Presidency in 1893. William McKinley twice chose the huge, high-ceilinged and many-balconied structure, and so

POLK HOME, COLUMBIA, TENNESSEE

James Polk gave the fan, below, bearing portraits of all the Presidents, including himself, to his wife for his inauguration. Sobersided Mrs. Polk disapproved of dancing, so at the more formal of the two Inaugural Balls the music was stopped while the Polks were there. At the other ball the orchestra ceased playing when the President and his lady arrived; but after fifteen minutes the dancers began to call for music, and the band complied.

Overleaf: The reception held after President Lincoln's second inaugural was open to the public and was not nearly as orderly as this picture represents. In a scene reminiscent of Andrew Jackson's first inauguration, hordes of tourists disregarded the arrangements made for them and swarmed through the open White House, shouldered aside the official guests, ate up food not intended for them, and—to Lincoln's amazement—stole silver and glassware and chunks of drapery as souvenirs. It is said that the President that night shook the hands of 6,000 people.

103

did Theodore Roosevelt and William Howard Taft. The Pension Building made second or third balls unnecessary: eighteen thousand people packed into the great hall to celebrate Taft's inauguration. But it was not uniformly popular among guests. General William Tecumseh Sherman, who knew about such things, was reported to have commented, "It's too bad the damn thing is fireproof!"

But the Pension Building and the vast body of humanity it could contain seemed to point up the problem with Inaugural Balls: they had become so big and cumbersome, so noisy, crowded, and uncomfortable that they hardly could have been called fun. They failed even as events where people could go to be seen. As a lady journalist wrote after Theodore Roosevelt's 1905 ball: "To the thousands all over the country who read accounts of the Inaugural Balls in their home paper, many with heart-burnings and envy of those who could and did attend, I would say: 'Don't! It is not worth it!' It is a most public affair, which anyone who can pay the price of entrance may attend. You may go dressed to be seen and to see, and accomplish neither because of the great crush. Dancing is almost an impossibility."

Woodrow Wilson not only eliminated the Pension Building as the quasi-official quarters of the Inaugural Ball; he eliminated the ball from his plans. A devoted, intensely private family man, Wilson detested having his wife and three daughters subjected to the sort of public gawking that had made, say, Alice Roosevelt's private life a public showcase (although Miss Roosevelt, later Mrs. Nicholas Longworth, did not seem to mind). The people apparently did not resent Wilson's decision, or think him a prig; his seriousness and sense of duty first were, after all, what they elected him for.

Now *no* ball threatened to become precedent. Actually, Warren G. Harding had intended to make his 1921 Inauguration Day as festive as a Fourth of July; but when a number of senators complained about the extravagance, Harding decided to cancel everything—even the parade. Thus a controversial administration and a remarkably frivolous era were ushered in with altogether inappropriate seriousness. Nor was there an

UPI

A beaming President and Mrs. Eisenhower pay a visit to the Mayflower Hotel—one of four ball sites—during the celebration that followed their second inauguration in 1957. It had been President Eisenhower who—after a long hiatus that began with Franklin Roosevelt's second term—made the ball again an important part of the inaugural.

official Inaugural Ball in 1925, when Calvin Coolidge was re-inaugurated. There was, however, an unofficial ball at the Mayflower Hotel, and Washington society responded to it as if it were official. But not Coolidge himself: exhausted by the ceremony, parade, and a private party held for him by some Massachusetts cronies, the President flopped down across his White House bed at nine-thirty in the evening and slept through the night.

Then there was the possibility that *that* might become precedent: unofficial balls not attended by Chief Executives. A ball was held in 1933, and Eleanor Roosevelt and many of her family were present, but Franklin D. Roosevelt was not. He had not fallen asleep, though. As the capital celebrated, he and his aide Louis Howe talked over the new administration's programs for the depression-stagnated nation. They were still chatting when the First Lady returned from the ball. No more balls were held for F.D.R.'s three subsequent inaugurals; and, the mood of the country being what it was each time, no one seemed to miss them.

But after World War II the ball was restored to its former status as a standard part of the Inauguration Day celebration. Dwight D. Eisenhower restored the double ball in 1953, attending each for half of the evening. In 1961, John F. Kennedy spread himself, his pretty wife, and his large and handsome entourage to a five-site ball; and in 1965, Lyndon, Lady Bird, Luci, and Lynda Johnson followed suit. The crush was still enormous, the dancing close to impossible. Still, everyone wanted to go.

There was an interesting twist to the preparations for the 1969 inaugural. All told, about two thousand people worked on the Inaugural Committee that planned all the official events of the inauguration. (Most of the workers were volunteers.) It is, of course, temporary work, and finding temporary work space for that many people is not easy. During the search, a General Services Administration official with a nose for history suggested that cavernous building on Fifth and G streets. It was a fine idea; and the Inaugural Committee moved its equipment and workers into the old Pension Building and got down to business.

The 1969 Inaugural Balls

At left, the scene at the Sheraton Park. Above, the Nixon party, visiting the several ball locations, included Tricia's escort, Douglas Rogers (center), son of the Secretary of State.

The capstone of the 1969 inauguration was the Inaugural Ball, held at six locations in Washington: the Mayflower, Statler Hilton, Washington Hilton, Shoreham, and Sheraton Park hotels, and—for the first time in inaugural history—the Smithsonian Institution's Museum of History and Technology.

Each of the ballrooms was decorated in white, gold, and silver. The orchestras of such as Duke Ellington, Sammy Kaye, Les Brown, and Guy Lombardo played for crowds that totaled about thirty thousand persons and were so thick that little dancing actually took place. "I thought this was supposed to be a ball," joked President Nixon as he surveyed the five thousand people packed into the museum hall. And the dance music, the exuberant guests, the military bands that saluted the President at each stop on his inauguration night tour combined to produce the happy cacophony so characteristic of these occasions.

Every ballroom had its particular attractions, but perhaps the most special was the museum, where two members-designate of the Cabinet, the diplomatic corps, all the Supreme Court justices, and the Apollo-8 astronauts, back from their moon circumnavigation, were in attendance.

There were hitches, as there always are. Visitors to the Vice President's Reception at the museum the day before the inauguration had taken away as souvenirs most of the carnations and roses in the flower arrangements, unaware that they were plucking the hall of decorations intended for the ball; repair of these ravages wore out a number of volunteers. At one hotel the temperature was cold enough to induce the beautifully gowned ladies to keep their furs on. But all in all this most glamorous of inauguration events was a great success. It takes months to work out the details of an Inaugural Ball, only a few hours to enjoy it, but to everyone attending it provides a lifetime of memories.

Mrs. Leslie Arends
Co-Chairman, Inaugural Ball Committee

Dinah Shore and vice-presidential staffer C. D. Ward.

At every ball site people surged forward for a handshake.

The President (above, at the right) happily greets and is greeted by the thousands of guests at the Mayflower Hotel.

Vibraphonist Lionel Hampton's band was popular.

Floor space was at a premium for those who came to dance.

At the left, President Nixon speaks at the Smithsonian ball. Behind him hangs the "Star Spangled Banner" of Francis Scott Key's anthem, the same flag that still flew over Fort McHenry, near Baltimore, on that September dawn in 1814 after a night's rocket bombardment by the British. Shown with the Nixons are, from left, Mrs. Mark Evans, Mrs. J. Willard Marriott, Mr. Marriott, Inaugural Committee Chairman, Inaugural Ball Chairman Mark Evans, Mrs. Nixon, Commerce Secretary Maurice Stans.

Martin Van Buren's hostess was his daughter-in-law, Angelica Singleton Van Buren of South Carolina. The President, a widower, owed her presence in the White House to a former First Lady, Dolley Madison, who had acted as matchmaker in the romance between her pretty young cousin and Abraham, the eldest of the four sons of President Van Buren.

As a national celebrity, only the Chief Executive himself outshines her. Within the awesome confines of the White House, some remarkable women have presided.

The President's Lady

By Amy La Follette Jensen

stood for a moment over the great brass seal, bearing the national coat of arms, which is sunk in the floor in the middle of the entrance hall. 'The Seal of the President of the United States,' I read around the border, and now—that meant my husband!" Thus did Helen Herron Taft describe her feelings as she entered the White House on Inauguration Day. Most presidential wives have shared her pride, but not all have experienced the same breathless anticipation of the four years ahead. "I had rather be a doorkeeper in the house of God, than live in that palace in Washington," commented Rachel Jackson—who, as fate would have it, died of a heart attack shortly before her husband assumed office. To Lucretia Garfield, the prospect seemed even frightening. "What a terrible responsibility to come to him—and to me," she exclaimed on election night of 1880. Some have shrunk from that responsibility, others have endured it bravely, and a few have thoroughly enjoyed their brief celebrity. Like it or not, the President's lady has become, over the years, a kind of unofficial officer of the government: presidential hostess, informal envoy, political campaigner. And wife, of course. Rutherford B. Hayes best expressed this aspect of her role. Referring to his wife, Lucy, he said, "Mrs. Hayes may not have much influence with Congress, but she has great influence with me." On these pages is a gallery of some of the great ladies who presided over the President's House—"that palace in Washington."

"I bear my drawing rooms, sometimes crowded, better than I expected," wrote Abigail Adams in one of her famous letters. As First Lady, John Adams' wife could not call up the ardor for pastimes purely social that she felt for a host of other interests: politics, morals, women's rights, the well-being of relatives. There were many who thought she even had the qualifications to be President.

AFTER A PAINTING BY ANDERS ZORN; WHITE HOUSE COLLECTION

Above: Both Julia Gardiner Tyler (left) and Frances Folsom Cleveland married Presidents many years their senior. In June of 1844 John Tyler, fifty-four and recently a widower, married a vivacious Long Island society belle of twenty-four. Julia thought the aging President handsome, his eloquence inspired; his pride in her grace and beauty was patent. Julia's few months in the White House as Tyler finished out William Henry Harrison's term was one long, showy paean to her husband—and to his major goal, the annexation of Texas. She set up a regular court, and received while seated on a dais, wearing a diadem-like headdress. Her final ball—three thousand came— was a triumph. Ten days later, less than a week before he left office, Tyler saw his Texas dreams come true. On June 2, 1886, Grover Cleveland married Frances Folsom—he was a bachelor of forty-nine, she was twenty-three—in the only presidential wedding ever held in the White House. Prying reporters followed the newlyweds on their honeymoon. Only that autumn, after the President, tears of anger in his eyes, publicly denounced the intrusions, did the press leave the First Family alone. The lovely Mrs. Cleveland was popular with the people. At White House receptions she greeted as many as nine thousand guests in an afternoon—with a fresh smile for each of them.

Left: Dolley Madison sent to Paris for her furbelows—laces and satins, snuffboxes and gauzy turbans—and her wines. She was not ravishing (Washington Irving accurately described her as "a fine, portly, buxom dame"), but her style was flamboyant, her energy boundless, her receptions fashionable. In sixteen years—eight presiding for the widowed Thomas Jefferson, eight as First Lady in her own right—she made herself perhaps the most famous White House hostess of all. She also had courage: she saved state papers—and a portrait of Washington—from the British in 1814.

Edith Carow Roosevelt thought she was one of the few women who had been happy in the White House. Harmony went hand in hand with the lovely, reserved wife of Theodore Roosevelt. The house rocked with activity. Five children romped through it from cellar to attic. Seventeen-year-old "Princess Alice" had a frenetic debut. The aging mansion itself underwent its first full-scale renovation —accompanied by major architectural changes—since its restoration after the War of 1812. The President practiced the strenuous life he advocated, with medicine ball, hiking, tennis, once even a jujitsu match in the East Room. But if Mrs. Roosevelt ever lost her composure, no one recorded the moment. Complex White House affairs ran without a hitch under her gentle but firm direction; she even found time to direct weekly meetings for Cabinet wives. Archie Butt, chronicler of the Roosevelt family, paid tribute to the First Lady's social talents: " . . . seven years in the White House without making a mistake!" She was Roosevelt's second wife; his first wife had died in 1884.

Scholarly President Woodrow Wilson, whose first wife had died during his first term, was enthralled by the handsome widow Edith Bolling Galt. She wore mauve to complement her violet eyes and she could lift his spirits with a look. The First Lady's secretary wrote of the President's second marriage, "She is the most wonderful wife in the world to a man who needs love and care more than any I have ever seen." Edith Wilson later gave proof of the depth of this observation. Upon Wilson's tragic collapse in 1919 she took charge not only of the sick room but, the evidence suggests, of presidential duties as well. For seventeen months the government was without an active leader, but Edith Wilson, protecting the President from the world, spoke in his name. She herself later called this period her stewardship; others had more critical names, like "Mrs. Wilson's Regency." Inevitably she was called the first woman President. No other First Lady except Mary Todd Lincoln had ever been so widely censured, although she was condemned for entirely different reasons.

Grace Goodhue Coolidge (left) had striking talents for the role of First Lady. To a stiff-faced administration her gregariousness and popularity brought a needed touch of informality and charm. She confessed to deriving genuine joy from the routine of her unpaid office. Chief Usher Ike Hoover recounted that "members of the household said she was ninety percent of the administration." The President adored his wife: he liked to see her well-dressed and often selected her clothes. But he also watched household details, checking menus and accounts daily. About the President's business, on the other hand, Mrs. Coolidge knew only what she read in the newspapers. When Coolidge made his famous "I do not choose to run" announcement in 1927, the first she knew anything of it was when a friend told her.

At the right are four of the five First Ladies who most recently occupied the White House before Pat Ryan Nixon, as they are depicted in their official portraits. Each of the five brought her own distinctive quality to the position. Eleanor Roosevelt (upper left) played probably as much of a political as a social role; she championed her husband's New Deal measures, traveled as his representative, and during World War II went as his emissary to war areas. Both Bess Wallace Truman (upper right) and Mamie Doud Eisenhower (lower left) brought a more restrained quality to the office. Mrs. Truman performed her official functions dutifully but sometimes with a touch of grimness that hinted she would rather be home. Mamie Eisenhower, on the other hand, had a warm and ready smile and moved through her duties with apparent ease, though she never got over a dislike for making speeches. She instituted her own press conferences at which, however, political questions were barred. Jacqueline Bouvier Kennedy (not shown because her portrait is unfinished) was admired for her youthful charm, but her most lasting impress was in her restoring of the White House interior to something like its original classical style. The dynamic Lady Bird Taylor Johnson (lower right) made beautification her special province; she not only pleaded its cause to the nation, but made many parks in Washington more colorful and attractive through her own personal attention.

121

Patricia Ryan Nixon

First Lady—it is a title of unique pre-eminence in our land, carrying with it responsibility and personal demand. Yet, Patricia Ryan Nixon wears the title with the quiet competence America has come to expect from the woman who has shared two decades of public life with a people who know her as Pat.

She is part of the America of which Walt Whitman and Carl Sandburg wrote—possessed of quiet strength; of dignity which is worn with naturalness; of patience which comes when life's goals are held comfortably in the mind and heart.

Pat Nixon shares with her husband an energetic and practical approach to life and politics. She believes that one gets out of life what one puts into it, and that the American dream is attainable because "people dream what they can achieve."

Since their marriage on June 21, 1940, she has been a steadfast partner in her husband's endeavors. When Richard Nixon was a struggling young lawyer, she supplemented the family income by teaching school. In later years, when her husband went on the campaign trail, she joined him there with equal dedication. Being busy has been not only a way of life to her, but a necessary component of happiness.

She was born in a Nevada mining town, of Irish-German parents, and grew up on a small truck farm in California, where she joined her father and brothers in harvesting the crops. When she was thirteen, her mother died, and Pat Nixon had to take over the responsibility of maintaining the family home. Five years later her father died, leaving her orphaned and on her own. She began a series of jobs that enabled her not only to take care of herself but also to save the money that would put her through the University of Southern California. Always, Pat Nixon found the adventure that compensated for the struggle. "It was a wonderful experience," she once said of her long years of deprivation and hard work. "It strengthened me."

After graduating cum laude with a Bachelor of Science degree, she accepted a teaching job at Whittier High School, where her extracurricular activities included rallying the pep band and cheerleaders for sports events. And because she had worked as a movie extra and bit player during college, she naturally turned to directing the school plays, as well as to community theater work. It was through her interest in the theater that she met her husband. The year was 1938, and Pat Ryan was chosen for the lead in a play put on by Whittier's Little Theater group. Richard Nixon, chosen to play "the guy who didn't get the girl," got the girl in real life. In fact, he proposed to her on their first meeting. Two years later they were married.

In the ensuing years, Mrs. Nixon served as mother and campaign worker, homemaker and counselor, as her husband progressed from congressman to United States senator to Vice President of the United States. She traveled nearly 150,000 miles to fifty-three countries during her husband's first term as Vice President. Visiting hospitals and schools by day and dining with heads of state in the evening, she was first the good-will ambassador, but also the student broadening her vistas, increasing her knowledge of the world and its people.

Her compassion and courage were never more evident than in the midst of a barrage of stones and shouted epithets in Caracas, Venezuela, in 1958. Walking up to a barricade that held back a mob of angry, spitting people, she reached out and gently grasped the hand of a girl who was one of the more vehement of the hate vendors. Suddenly tears welled up in the girl's eyes and she turned away ashamed.

The First Lady has imparted to her two daughters the qualities of honesty and of consideration for others. She has sustained and encouraged her husband during times when defeat and disappointment struck heavy blows and politics was no longer a joyous adventure. Now a new drama unfolds and she stands ready to play another role.

Gerry Van der Heuvel
Press Secretary to the First Lady

Martha Washington

Abigail Adams

Shawl worn by Martha Randolph
daughter of Thomas Jefferson

Dolley Madison

Gowns of the First Ladies

The gowns depicted on this and the next three pages were worn by the forty-one First Ladies—the wives or official hostesses of the Presidents. Most were those worn at Inaugural Balls. They are now on public display in the First Ladies' Hall of the Smithsonian Institution in Washington. These renderings were made expressly for the Inaugural Committee and this book by artist Cal Sacks.

Elizabeth K. Monroe

Marie M. Gouverneur
daughter of James Monroe

Louisa Catherine Adams

Emily Donelson
niece of Andrew Jackson

Sarah Y. Jackson
daughter-in-law of Andrew Jackson

Angelica L. Van Buren
daughter-in-law of Martin Van Buren

Jane I. Findlay
hostess for William H. Harrison

Julia Gardiner Tyler

Sarah C. Polk

Betty T. Bliss
daughter of Zachary Taylor

Abigail Powers Fillmore

Jane Appleton Pierce

Harriet Lane
niece of James Buchanan

Mary Todd Lincoln

Martha J. Patterson
daughter of Andrew Johnson

Julia Dent Grant

Lucy Webb Hayes

Lucretia R. Garfield

Mary A. McElroy
sister of Chester Arthur

Rose Cleveland
sister of Grover Cleveland

Caroline Scott Harrison

Mary H. McKee
daughter of Benjamin Harrison

Frances Folsom Cleveland

Ida Saxton McKinley

Edith Carow Roosevelt

Helen Herron Taft

Ellen Axson Wilson

Edith Bolling Wilson

Florence Kling Harding

Grace Goodhue Coolidge

Lou Henry Hoover

Anna Eleanor Roosevelt

Bess Wallace Truman

Mamie Doud Eisenhower

Jacqueline Bouvier Kennedy

Claudia Taylor Johnson

Patricia Ryan Nixon

The President's seal and his coat of arms (the portion within the circlet of stars, above) were both designed in 1880 and first used by President Rutherford B. Hayes. However, the coat of arms violated the rules of heraldry because the eagle faced toward its left instead of its right, and this was not corrected until 1945, at which time a circlet of stars, one for each state, was added to the coat of arms. The first President's flag was designed in 1916 and modified in 1945; it consists today of the coat of arms— the eagle and ring of fifty stars—on a field of deep blue.

The Power and the Burden

GEORGE WASHINGTON
1789–1797

The ceremony of inauguration early became symbolic of a national continuity that existed in spite of partisan politics. Thomas Jefferson set the tone in his famous first inaugural—"We are all republicans, we are all federalists." Margaret Bayard Smith, wife of a Republican editor, described the event in a letter to her sister-in-law.

Let me write to you my dear Susan, e'er that glow of enthusiasm has fled, which now animates my feelings; let me congratulate not only you, but all my fellow citizens, on an event which will have so auspicious an influence on their political welfare. I have this morning witnessed one of the most interesting scenes, a free people can ever witness. The changes of administration, which in every government and in every age have most generally been epochs of confusion, villainy and bloodshed, in this our happy country take place without any species of distraction, or disorder. This day, has one of the most amiable and worthy men taken that seat to which he was called by the voice of his country. I cannot describe the agitation I felt, while I looked around on the various multitude and while I listened to an address, containing principles the most correct, sentiments the most liberal, and wishes the most benevolent, conveyed in the most appropriate and elegant language and in a manner mild as it was firm. If doubts of the integrity and talents of Mr. Jefferson ever existed in the minds of any one, methinks this address must forever eradicate them.

JOHN ADAMS
1797–1801

Normally the national momentum overcame even the bitterest of election campaigns; still there were those who sensed a spirit of revolution in certain inaugurations— those of Jefferson and Andrew Jackson being good examples. The following was written by Arthur J. Stansbury for the May, 1851, edition of Arthur's Home Gazette.

To us, who had witnessed the quiet and orderly period of the Adams' administration, it seemed as if half the nation had rushed at once into the Capital. It was like the inundation of the northern barbarians into Rome, save that the tumultuous tide came in from a different point of the compass. The West and the South seemed to have precipitated themselves upon the North and overwhelmed it. On that memorable occasion you might tell a "Jackson man" almost as far as you could see him. Their every motion seemed to cry out "victory!" Strange faces filled every public place, and every face seemed to bear defiance on its brow. It appeared to me that every Jackson editor in the country was on the spot. They swarmed, especially in the lobbies of the House, an expectant host, a sort of Praetorian band, which, having borne in upon their shields their idolized leader, claimed the reward of the hard-fought contest. His quarters were assailed, surrounded, hemmed in, so that it was an achievement to get into his presence. On the morning of the inauguration, the vicinity of the Capitol was like a great agitated sea; every avenue to the fateful spot was blocked up with people, in so much that the legitimate procession which

THOMAS JEFFERSON
1801–1809

accompanied the President-elect could scarce make its way to the eastern portico, where the ceremony was to be performed. To repress the crowd in front, a ship's cable was stretched across about two-thirds of the way up the long flight of steps by which the Capitol is approached on that side, but it seemed, at times, as if even this would scarce prove sufficient to restrain the eagerness of the multitude, every man of whom seemed bent on the glory of shaking the President's hand. Never can I forget the spectacle which presented itself on every side, nor the electrifying moment when the eager, expectant eyes of that vast and motley multitude caught sight of the tall and imposing form of their adored leader, as he came forth between the columns of the portico, the color of the whole mass changed, as if by miracle; all hats were off at once, and the dark tint which usually pervades a mixed map of men was turned, as by a magic wand, into the bright hue of ten thousand upturned and exultant human faces, radiant with sudden joy. The peal of shouting that arose rent the air, and seemed to shake the very ground. But when the Chief Justice took his place and commenced the brief ceremony of administering the oath of office, it quickly sank into comparative silence; and as the new President proceeded to read his inaugural address, the stillness gradually increased; but all efforts to hear him, beyond a brief space immediately around, were utterly vain.

JAMES MADISON
1809–1817

Inaugural Addresses were sometimes greeted by partisan attacks, but if modern Americans were to pick the speech least likely to attract such fire and most likely to receive universal praise, it would probably be Lincoln's moving second inaugural, in which he called for "malice toward none, . . . charity for all." Yet the Chicago Times of March 6, 1865, saw in it nothing to applaud, everything to blame.

The inaugural addresses of the past presidents of the United States are among the best of our state papers. Profound in their comprehension of the principles of the government; exalted in their aspirations; magnificent in their patriotism; broad, liberal, catholic in their nationality; elevated in their literary style,—they will stand forever as the grandest monuments of American statesmanship. They were consonant with the national character. They were the natural product of the glorious years in which the republic grew from its revolutionary birth to be the most powerful nation on the face of the earth.

Contrast with these the inaugural address of Abraham Lincoln, delivered in the city of Washington on Saturday, and printed in these columns this morning! "What a fall was there, my countrymen." Was there ever such a coming out of the little end of the horn? Was ever a nation, once great, so belittled? Is such another descent of record in the history of any people?

We had looked for something thoroughly Lincolnian, but we did not forsee a thing so much more Lincolnian than anything that has gone before it. We did not conceive it possible that even Mr. Lincoln could produce a paper so slip shod, so loose-joined, so puerile, not alone in literary construction, but in its ideas, its sentiments, its grasp. He has outdone himself. He has literally come out of the little end of his own horn. By the side of it, mediocrity is superb.

Let us trust in Heaven that it is not typical of our national degeneracy. Great, indeed, is our fall if the distance be so far as this performance of yesterday is beneath the statesmanship of former times.

Its appearance did not excite the slightest public interest in this city. It fell as if still-born. There would seem to have been some popular premonition of what was

JAMES MONROE
1817–1825

131

coming. The opportunity was a grand one to withdraw for a moment the earnest gaze of the country from the passing stupendous events in the military field, and attract it to the central figure which has power to direct those events. How incompetent was Mr. Lincoln to embrace that opportunity we do most painfully behold.

"He . . . shall take Care that the Laws be faithfully executed . . ."
—The Constitution, Article II.

JOHN QUINCY ADAMS
1825–1829

ANDREW JACKSON
1829–1837

MARTIN VAN BUREN
1837–1841

Presidents were charged by the Constitution to enforce federal statutes. In 1794, after Congress had passed a law calling for an excise tax on whiskey, Pennsylvania "whiskey boys" began an armed rebellion. It was an important test of federal power. President Washington warned the tax dodgers and then, in a proclamation (below), called out the militia. The federal troops marched into Pennsylvania, where the rebels gave up the struggle without a gun being fired. Of the many men who had engaged in the uprising, only two went to jail, and Washington subsequently pardoned both of them.

Whereas, from a hope that the combinations against the Constitution and laws of the United States, in certain of the Western counties of Pennsylvania, would yield to time and reflection, I thought it sufficient, in the first instance, rather to take measures for calling forth the militia than immediately to embody them; but the moment is now come, when the overtures of forgiveness, with no other condition than a submission to law, have been only partially accepted; when every form of conciliation not inconsistent with the being of Government has been adopted, without effect . . . when it is manifest, that violence would continue to be exercised upon every attempt to enforce the laws; when, therefore, Government is set at defiance, the contest being whether a small proportion of the United States shall dictate to the whole Union, and, at the expense of those who desire peace, indulge a desperate ambition;

Now, therefore, I, GEORGE WASHINGTON, President of the United States, in obedience to that high and irresistible duty, consigned to me by the Constitution, "to take care that the laws be faithfully executed;" . . . resolved, in perfect reliance on that gracious Providence which so signally displays its goodness towards this country, to reduce the refractory to a due subordination to the laws; do hereby declare and make known, that, with a satisfaction which can be equalled only by the merits of the militia summoned into service from the States of New Jersey, Pennsylvania, Maryland, and Virginia, I have received intelligence of their patriotic alacrity, in obeying the call of the present, though painful, yet commanding necessity; that a force, which, according to every reasonable expectation, is adequate to the exigency, is already in motion to the scene of disaffection; that those who have confided or shall confide in the protection of Government, shall meet full succor under the standard and from the arms of the United States; that those who having offended against the laws have since entitled themselves to indemnity, will be treated with the most liberal good faith, if they shall not have forfeited their claim by any subsequent conduct, and that instructions are given accordingly. . . .

On occasion Presidents have been faced with the necessity of executing laws of which they didn't approve. Millard Fillmore supported and signed the series of bills since known collectively as the Compromise of 1850; he believed the Compromise was the best way to achieve permanent intersectional peace over the slavery issue. One of the new laws demanded that fugitive slaves be returned to their owners, and though Fillmore didn't like it and knew it was unpopular in the North, he felt bound to enforce it, as he wrote Secretary of State Daniel Webster in October of 1850.

. . . I have received a copy of Judge Woodbury's charge on the Fugitive Slave Law, and the Report of Judge Grier's opinion in a case before him, all manfully sustaining the constitutionality of the law, and manifesting a determined resolution to carry it out. I have also just received a joint letter from Judge Grier and Judge Keane, stating that a case has occurred before a commission in Pennsylvania where the execution of a warrant under that act was "forcibly and successfully resisted; the posse summoned to aid the officer having refused to act," and "inquiring whether upon the recurrence of an obstruction to his Process he will be entitled to call for the aid of such troops of the United States as may be accessible."

This you perceive presents a very grave and delicate question. I have not yet had time to look into it and regret much that so many of my Cabinet are absent, and especially yourself and the attorney general. These judges ask for a general order authorizing the employment of the troops in such an emergency; and I am disposed to exert whatever power I possess under the Constitution and laws, in enforcing this observance. I know no higher law that conflicts with it; and that Constitution says, "the President shall take care that the laws be faithfully executed." I mean at every sacrifice and at every hazard to perform my duty. The Union must and shall be preserved, and this can only be done, by a faithful and impartial administration of the laws. I can not doubt that in these sentiments you are with me. And if you have occasion to speak I hope you will give no encouragement, even by implication, to any resistance to the law. Nullification can not and will not be tolerated. . . .

"Every Bill which shall have passed the House of Representatives and the Senate, shall, before it become a Law, be presented to the President . . . If he approve he shall sign it, but if not he shall return it, with his Objections to that House in which it shall have originated . . ."
—The Constitution, Article I

John Tyler vetoed ten bills in his term as William Henry Harrison's emergency successor. It was the greatest number of negatives for a one-term executive until Andrew Johnson's Presidency, and Tyler was quickly nicknamed Old Veto. Here he presents an able defense of the constitutional provision and his use of it.

133

. . . I readily admit that whilst the qualified *veto* with which the Chief Magistrate is invested should be regarded and was intended by the wise men who made it a part of the Constitution as a great conservative principle of our system . . . yet it is a power which ought to be most cautiously exerted, and perhaps never except in a case eminently involving the public interest or one in which the oath of the President, acting upon his conviction, both mental and moral, imperiously requires its exercise. In such a case he has no alternative. He must either exert the negative power intrusted to him by the Constitution chiefly for its own preservation, protection, and defense or commit an act of gross moral turpitude. Mere regard to the will of a majority must not in a constitutional republic like ours control this sacred and solemn duty of a sworn officer. The Constitution itself I regard and cherish as the embodied and written will of the whole people of the United States. It is their fixed and fundamental law, which they unanimously prescribe to the public functionaries, their mere trustees and servants. This *their* will and the law which *they* have given us as the rule of our action have no guard, no guaranty of preservation, protection, and defense, but the oaths which it prescribes to the public officers, the sanctity with which they shall religiously observe those oaths, and the patriotism with which the people shall shield it by their own sovereign will, which has made the Constitution supreme. It must be exerted against the will of a mere representative majority or not at all. It is alone in pursuance of that will that any measure can reach the President, and to say that because a majority in Congress have passed a bill he should therefore sanction it is to abrogate the power altogether and to render its insertion in the Constitution a work of absolute supererogation. . . .

"The President shall be Commander in Chief of the Army and Navy of the United States . . ."
—The Constitution, Article II

Chief Executives have almost never exercised their responsibility for the armed forces as battlefield commanders. James Madison did, during the British drive on Washington in 1814. It was an extraordinary situation; for example, Secretary of State James Monroe was operating as a scout for his commander in chief, on horseback tracking the enemy troops as they neared Bladensburg, Maryland, a few miles from the capital. Madison's account follows.

In the morning, a note, by an express from General Winder was handed me. It was addressed to the Secretary of War. Not doubting the urgency of the occasion, I opened and read it, and it went on immediately by the Express to Gen. Armstrong. . . . Finding by the note that the General requested the speediest counsel, I proceeded to his Head Quarters on the Eastern Branch, trusting for notice to the Secretary of War to follow, to the note from Winder. On my reaching his quarters, we were successively joined by the Secretary of State (who soon with our approbation repaired to Bladensburg) the Secretary of the Navy, and Mr. Rush, the Attorney General. After an hour or so, the Secretary of the Treasury arrived, and quickly after the Secretary of War. The latter had been impatiently expected, and

MILLARD FILLMORE
1850–1853

FRANKLIN PIERCE
1853–1857

JAMES BUCHANAN
1857–1861

ABRAHAM LINCOLN
1861–1865

surprize at his delay manifested. Gen. Winder was, at the moment setting off to hurry on the troops to Bladensburg in consequence of certain intelligence that the Enemy had taken that direction. . . . On Gen. Armstrong's coming into the room, he was informed of the certain march of the enemy for Bladensburg, and of what had passed before his arrival; and he was asked whether he had any arrangement or advice to offer in the emergency. He said he had not; adding, that as the battle would be between Militia and regular troops, the former would be beaten.

On coming out of the house and mounting our horses, the Secretary of the Treasury, who though in a very languid state of health had turned out to join us, observed to me privately that he was grieved to see the great reserve of the Secretary of War (he lodged in the same house with him), who was taking no part on so critical an occasion; that he found him under the impression, that as the means of defending the District had been committed to Gen. Winder, it might not be delicate to intrude his opinions without the approbation of the President; tho' with that approbation he was ready to give any aid he could. . . . I told him I could scarcely conceive it possible that Gen. Armstrong could have so misconstrued his functions and duty as Secretary of War; that he could not but know that any proper directions from him would receive any sanction that might be necessary from the Executive; not doubt that any suggestions or advice from him to Gen. Winder would be duly attended to (in this case it had been requested in writing) I told Mr. C. that I would speak to the Secretary of War explicitly on the subject; and accordingly turning my horse to him, expressed to him my concern and surprize at the reserve he shewed at the present crisis, and at the scruples I understood he had at offering his advice or opinions; . . . that at such a juncture it was to be expected that he should omit nothing within the proper agency of Secretary of War, towards the public defence; and that I thought it proper particularly that he should proceed to Bladensburg and give any aid to Gen. Winder that he could; observing that if any difficulty on the score of authority should arise, which was not likely, I should be near at hand to remove it (it was my purpose in case there should be time, to have the members of the Cabinet together in Bladensburg, where it was expected Gen. Winder would be, and in consultation with him to decide on the arrangements suited to the posture of things). . . . The Secretary of War set off without delay to Bladensburg.

After a short turn to the Marine barracks whither the Secretary of the Navy had gone, I mentioned to Mr. Rush who was with me my purpose of going to Bladensburg and my object in so doing. He readily accompanied me. On approaching the Town, we learned from William Simmons, that Winder was not there, and that the enemy were entering it. . . . I asked the [Secretary of War] whether he had spoken with Gen. Winder on the subject of his arrangements and views. He said he had not. I remarked that tho' there was so little time for it, it was possible he might offer some advice or suggestion that might not be too late, to be turned to account; on which he rode up to the General as I did myself. The unruliness of my horse prevented me from joining in the short conversation that took place. When it was over, I asked Gen. Armstrong whether he had seen occasion to suggest any improvement in any part of the arrangements. He said that he had not; that from his view of them they appeared to be as good as circumstances admitted.

When the Battle had decidedly commenced, I observed to the Secretary of War and Secretary of State that it would be proper to withdraw to a position in the rear, where we could act according to circumstances; leaving military movements now to the military functionaries who were responsible for them. This we did, Mr. Rush soon joining us. When it became manifest that the battle was lost; Mr. Rush accompanying me, I fell down into the road leading to the city and returned to it.

135

ANDREW JOHNSON
1865–1869

ULYSSES SIMPSON GRANT
1869–1877

The role of commander in chief has always involved difficult questions. Below, Abraham Lincoln—then a congressman from Illinois—discusses one of them in a letter to a friend about President Polk's actions in the Mexican War. Polk had ordered Zachary Taylor's army to move into disputed territory near the Rio Grande; several battles against the Mexicans had followed; and then Congress declared war.

. . . Let me first state what I understand to be your position. It is, that if it shall become *necessary, to repel invasion,* the President may, without violation of the Constitution, cross the line, and *invade* the territory of another country; and that whether such *necessity* exists in any given case, the President is to be the *sole* judge.

Before going further, consider well whether this is, or is not your position. If it is, it is a position that neither the President himself, nor any friend of his, so far as I know, has ever taken. Their only positions are first, that the soil was *ours* where hostilities commenced, and second, that whether it was rightfully *ours* or not, *Congress had annexed it,* and the President, for that reason was bound to defend it, both of which are as clearly proved to be false in fact, as you can prove that your house is not mine. That soil was not ours; and Congress did not annex or attempt to annex it. But to return to your position: Allow the President to invade a neighboring nation, whenever *he* shall deem it necessary to repel an invasion, and you allow him to do so, *whenever he may choose to say* he deems it necessary for such purpose—and you allow him to make war at pleasure. Study to see if you can fix *any limit* to his power in this respect, after you have given him so much as you propose. If, to-day, he should choose to say he thinks it necessary to invade Canada, to prevent the British from invading us, how could you stop him? You may say to him, "I see no probability of the British invading us" but he will say to you "be silent; I see it, if you dont."

The provision of the Constitution giving the war-making power to Congress, was dictated, as I understand it, by the following reasons. Kings had always been involving and impoverishing their people in wars, pretending generally, if not always, that the good of the people was the object. This, our Convention understood to be the most oppressive of all Kingly oppressions; and they resolved to so frame the Constitution that *no one man* should hold the power of bringing this oppression upon us. But your view destroys the whole matter, and places our President where kings have always stood. . . .

"He . . . shall nominate, and by and with the Advice and Consent of the Senate, shall appoint Ambassadors, other public Ministers and Consuls, Judges of the supreme Court, and all other officers of the United States, whose Appointments are not herein otherwise provided for . . ."
—The Constitution, Article II

The appointing power has been as much of a problem as an aid to Presidents. The following excerpts were written in 1847 and 1933, the first by President Polk in his diary and the second by H. L. Mencken in the Baltimore Evening Sun.

RUTHERFORD BIRCHARD HAYES
1877–1881

. . . Many persons, members of Congress and others, called today; all of them or nearly all on what they may regard as the patriotic, but which I consider the contemptible business of seeking office for themselves or their friends. The passion for office and the number of unworthy persons who seek to live on the public is increasing beyond former example, and I now predict that no President of the United States of either party will ever again be reëlected. The reason is that the patronage of the government will destroy the popularity of any President, however well he may administer the government. The office-seekers have become so numerous that they hold the balance of power between the two great parties of the country. In every appointment which the President makes he disappoints half a dozen applicants and their friends, who, actuated by selfish and sordid motives, will prefer any other candidate in the next election, while the person appointed attributes the appointment to his own superior merit and does not even feel obliged by it. . . . Another great difficulty in making appointments which the President encounters is that he cannot tell upon what recommendations to rely. Members of Congress and men of high station in the country sign papers of recommendation, either from interested personal motives or without meaning what they say, and thus the President is often imposed on, and induced to make bad appointments. When he does so the whole responsibility falls on himself, while those who have signed papers of recommendation and misled him, take special care never to avow the agency they have had in the matter, or to assume any part of the responsibility. I have had some remarkable instances of this during my administration . . . shortly after the commencement of my administration I made an appointment upon the letter of recommendation of a Senator. I sent the nomination to the Senate at the last session and it was rejected, and, as I learned, at the instance of the same Senator who had made the recommendation. A few days afterwards the Senator called to recommend another person for the same office. I said to him, well, you rejected the man I nominated; O yes, he replied, he was without character and wholly unqualified. I then asked him if he knew upon whose recommendation I had appointed him, to which he replied that he did not. I then handed to him his own letter and told him that was the recommendation upon which I had appointed him. He appeared confused and replied, Well, we are obliged to recommend our constituents when they apply to us. . . .

JAMES ABRAM GARFIELD
1881

I am not a Roosevelt fanatic, certainly, though I voted for the right hon. gentleman last November, and even printed a few discreet pieces arguing that he might be worse. But it must be manifest that, in any situation as full of dynamite as the present one, it is a great advantage to have a leader who can devote his whole time and thought to the problems before him, without any consideration of extraneous matters. Yet that is precisely what, under our present system, a President cannot do. He is forced, at every moment of his first term, to remember that he may be thrown out at the end of it, and it is thus no wonder that his concern often wobbles him, and makes him a too easy mark for the political blackmailers who constantly threaten him.

If his term were unlimited, or limited only by his good behavior—in brief, if he were in the position of an elected King—he would get rid of all this nuisance, and be free to apply himself to his business. I believe that any man, under such circumstances, would do immensely better than he could possibly do under the present system. And I believe that Dr. Roosevelt, in particular, would be worth at least ten times what he is worth now, for he is a good enough politician to know that his

CHESTER ALAN ARTHUR
1881–1885

GROVER CLEVELAND
1885–1889, 1893–1897

current high and feverish popularity cannot last, democracy being what it is, and that the only way he can save himself in 1936 is by forgetting the Depression once or twice a day, and applying himself to very practical politics.

What this division of aim and interest amounts to is shown brilliantly by some of his appointments. He has made a plain effort to surround himself with men in whose competence and good faith he can put his trust, but he has been forced by the exigencies of his uncomfortable situation to give a number of important posts to political plugs of the most depressing sort. These plugs were too powerful to be flouted, and now that they are in office they are even more powerful than before. If they remain they will disgrace the administration soon or late, and if they are turned out they will imperil it in 1936. An elected King could rid himself of them at once, and they could do him no damage, now or hereafter.

"He shall have Power, by and with the Advice and Consent of the Senate, to make Treaties . . ."
—The Constitution, Article II

BENJAMIN HARRISON
1889–1893

One of the most bitter and prolonged contests between the executive and legislative branches involved the Treaty of Versailles and America's participation in the League of Nations. In the view of many key members of the Senate, the pact would diminish the Senate's power over foreign affairs. Here, Idaho's "irreconcilable" Senator William E. Borah argues against the treaty.

When the league shall have been formed, we shall be a member of what is known as the council of the league. Our accredited representative will sit in judgment with the accredited representatives of the other members of the league to pass upon the concerns not only of our country but of all Europe and all Asia and the entire world. Our accredited representatives will be members of the assembly. They will sit there to represent the judgment of these 110,000,000 people . . . just as we are accredited here to represent our constituencies. We cannot send our representatives to sit in council with the representatives of the other great nations of the world with mental reservations as to what we shall do in case their judgment shall not be satisfactory to us. If we go to the council or the assembly with any other purpose than that of complying in good faith and in absolute integrity with all upon which the council or the assembly may pass, we shall soon return to our country with our self-respect forfeited and the public opinion of the world condemnatory.

Why need you gentlemen across the aisle worry about a reservation here or there when we are sitting in the council and in the assembly and bound by every obligation in morals, which the President said was supreme above that of law, to comply with the judgment that our representative and the other representatives finally form? Shall we go there . . . to sit in judgment, and in case that judgment works for peace join with our allies, but in case it works for war withdraw our cooperation? How long would we stand as we now stand, a great Republic commanding the respect and holding the leadership of the world, if we should adopt any such course? . . .

We have said . . . that we would not send our troops abroad without the consent

WILLIAM McKINLEY
1897–1901

138

of Congress. Pass by now for a moment the legal proposition. If we create executive functions, the Executive will perform those functions without the authority of Congress. Pass that question by and go to the other question. [Suppose that] our members of the council are there. Our members of the assembly are there. Article 11 is complete, and it authorizes the league, a member of which is our representative, to deal with matters of peace and war, and the league through its council and its assembly deals with the matter, and our accredited representative joins with the others in deciding upon a certain course, which involves a question of sending troops. What will the Congress of the United States do? What right will it have left, except the bare technical right to refuse, which as a moral proposition it will not dare to exercise? Have we not been told day by day for the last nine months that the Senate of the United States, a coordinate part of the treaty-making power, should accept this league as it was written because the wise men sitting at Versailles had so written it, and has not every possible influence and every source of power in public opinion been organized and directed against the Senate to compel it to do that thing? How much stronger will be the moral compulsion upon the Congress of the United States when we ourselves have indorsed the proposition of sending our accredited representatives there to vote for us?

"The President . . . shall be removed from Office on Impeachment for, and Conviction of, Treason, Bribery, or other high Crimes and Misdemeanors."
—The Constitution, Article II

Though the threat has been raised more than once, only one President has actually been impeached by the House and brought to trial before the Senate, and even that event was engineered by Congress for political reasons. Having made it a "high misdemeanor" for Union Democrat Andrew Johnson to remove any of his predecessor's Cabinet members without the Senate's approval, the Radical Republicans impeached the President when he showed his determination to assert the traditional prerogatives of his office and have his own Cabinet. The coup nearly succeeded, the Senate failing by the margin of a single vote to convict Johnson and elevate their own presiding officer to the powers and duties of the Presidency. Below, Senator Edmund G. Ross of Kansas—the only man whose intent was not known before the balloting and whose vote the Radicals had to have—describes the scene in the Senate.

. . . That day, May 15, 1868, was fateful. There had been none such in nearly a hundred years of the history of the Government. It was to determine judicially a question of varying phases which had never before been brought for solution in the courts—what should constitute "high crimes and misdemeanors in office" on the part of the National Executive; what latitude should be allowed him in the expression of personal opinion in his differences with co-ordinate branches of the Government; how far he might lawfully go in the exercise of his personal judgment in the administration of the powers and duties of his great office; whether his oath of office permitted him to interpret the Constitution for himself in the absence and

anticipation of judicial determination, or whether he should be governed by Congressional interpretation of that instrument. In a large sense, the independence of the executive office as a co-ordinate branch of the Government was on trial. . . .

The hours seemed to pass with oppressive tedium awaiting the time for the assembling of the Senate and the beginning of the vote. It came at last, and found the galleries thronged to their utmost with a brilliant and eager auditory. Tickets of admission were at an enormous premium. Every chair on the floor was filled with a Senator, a Cabinet officer, a member of the President's counsel, or a representative, for the House had adjourned and its anxious members had at once thronged to the Senate chamber. Every foot of available standing room in the area and about the senatorial seats was occupied. . . .

Pages were flitting from place to place with messages. . . . Little groups were gathered here and there in subdued conversation, discussing the situation and the probable result and its attendant consequences. The intensity of public interest was increased by the general impression that the entire official incumbency and patronage of the Government in all its departments, financial and political, had been pledged in advance and on condition of the removal of the President. . . .

The Chief Justice, with apparent emotion, propounded the query, "How say you, Senator Ross, is the respondent, Andrew Johnson, guilty or not guilty under this article?"

At this point the intensity with which the gaze of the audience was centred upon the figure then on the floor was beyond description or comparison. Hope and fear seemed blended in every face, instantaneously alternating, some with revengeful hate predominating as in the mind's eye they saw their dreams of success, of place, and triumph dashed to earth; others lighted with hope that the President would be relieved of the charges against him, and things remain as they were. Not only were the occupants of the galleries bending forward in intense and breathless silence and anxiety to catch the verdict, but the Senators in their seats leaned over their desks, many with hand to ear, that not a syllable or intonation in the utterance of the verdict should be lost.

Conscious that I was at that moment the focus of all eyes, and conscious also of the far-reaching effect, especially upon myself, of the vote I was about to give, it is something more than a simile to say that I almost literally looked down into my open grave. Friends, position, fortune, everything that makes life desirable to an ambitious man, were about to be swept away by the breath of my mouth, perhaps forever. Realizing the tremendous responsibility which an untoward combination of conditions seemed to have put upon me, it is not strange that my answer was carried waveringly over the air and failed to reach the limits of the audience, or that a repetition was called for by distant Senators on the opposite side of the chamber. Then the verdict came—"Not guilty"—in a voice that could not be misunderstood. . . .

"Our Country is an extensive one. We must either then renounce the blessings of the Union, or provide an Executive with sufficient vigor to pervade every part of it."
—Gouverneur Morris, at the Constitutional Convention

The enormous powers of the Presidency have been viewed and used in many different ways by the individuals who have held the office. Below, Theodore Roosevelt writes about his attitudes in a letter to historian George Trevelyan; one of the questions under discussion was whether T.R. should run for a third term.

. . . Now, my ambition is that, in however small a way, the work I do shall be along the Washington and Lincoln Lines. While President I have *been* President, emphatically; I have used every ounce of power there was in the office and I have not cared a rap for the criticisms of those who spoke of my "usurpation of power"; for I knew that the talk was all nonsense and that there was no usurpation. I believe that the efficiency of this Government depends upon its possessing a strong central executive, and wherever I could establish a precedent for strength in the executive, as I did for instance as regards external affairs in the case of sending the fleet around the world, taking Panama, settling affairs of Santo Domingo and Cuba; or as I did in internal affairs in settling the anthracite coal strike, in keeping order in Nevada this year when the Federation of Miners threatened anarchy, or as I have done in bringing the big corporations to book—why, in all these cases I have felt not merely that my action was right in itself, but that in showing the strength of, or in giving strength to, the executive, I was establishing a precedent of value. I believe in a strong executive; I believe in power; but I believe that responsibility should go with power, and that it is not well that the strong executive should be a perpetual executive. Above all and beyond all I believe as I have said before that the salvation of this country depends upon Washington and Lincoln representing the type of leader to which we are true. I hope that in my acts I have been a good President, a President who has deserved well of the Republic; but most of all, I believe that whatever value my service may have comes even more from what I *am* than from what I *do*. I may be mistaken, but it is my belief that the bulk of my countrymen, the men whom Abraham Lincoln called "the plain people"—the farmers, mechanics, small tradesmen, hard-working professional men—feel that I am in a peculiar sense their President, that I represent the democracy in somewhat the fashion that Lincoln did, that is, not in any demagogic way but with the sincere effort to stand for a government by the people and for the people. Now the chief service I can render these plain people who believe in me is, not to destroy their ideal of me.

H. Parker Willis, Calvin Coolidge's cousin, described a conversation they had in 1928. At the time the total of brokers' loans to stock speculators had grown so large that wise heads in the financial world were worried about the stability of the market, but the President continued to reassure the public that all was well.

After the business which we had had in hand had been disposed of, Mr. Coolidge invited me to come back to luncheon. I did so, and after luncheon sat down with him in his study for a while, and he asked me a number of questions about pending financial affairs. It so happened that two or three days before that he had given out at the White House a statement that brokers' loans were not at all too large. On the occasion of this visit to Washington I had been testifying before the Senate committee that I thought they were very much too large. President Coolidge . . . remarked that my opinion had seemed to show a great difference from his, but he added:

"If I were to give my own personal opinion about it, I should say that any loan made for gambling in stocks was an 'excessive loan.'"

I replied: "I wish very much, Mr. President, that you had been willing to say that instead of making the public statement you did."

"Why did you say that?" Mr. Coolidge queried.

"Simply because I think it would have had a tremendous effect in repressing an unwholesome speculation, with which, I now see, you have no sympathy."

Mr. Coolidge thought this over for a moment or so and then he said: "Well, I regard myself as the representative of the government and not as an individual. When technical matters come up I feel called on to refer them to the proper department of the government which has some information about them and then, unless there is some good reason, I use this information as a basis for whatever I have to say; but that does not prevent me from thinking what I please as an individual."

Seeking the Presidency in 1968, Richard Nixon devoted a major speech to his concept of the office. Excerpts from that address follow.

The President is trusted, not to follow the fluctuations of the public-opinion polls, but to bring his own best judgment to bear on the best *ideas* his administration can muster.

There are occasions on which a President must take unpopular measures.

But his responsibility does not stop there. The President has a duty to decide, but the people have a right to know why. The President has a responsibility to tell them—to lay out all the facts, and to explain not only why he chose as he did but also what it means for the future. Only through an open, candid dialogue with the people can a President maintain his trust and his leadership. . . .

When we think of leadership, we commonly think of persuasion. But the coin of leadership has another side.

In order to lead, a President today must listen. And in this time of searching and uncertainty, government must learn to listen in new ways.

A President has to hear not only the clamorous voices of the organized, but also the quiet voices, the *inner voices*—the voices that speak through the silences, and that speak from the heart and the conscience.

These are the voices that carry the real meaning and the real message of America.

He's got to articulate these voices so that they can be heard, rather than being lost in the wail and the bellow of what too often passes today for public discourse. He must be, in the words of Woodrow Wilson, "the spokesman for the real sentiment and purpose of the country."

The President is the one official who represents every American—rich and poor, privileged and underprivileged. He represents those whose misfortunes stand in dramatic focus, and also the great, quiet forgotten majority—the non-shouters and the non-demonstrators, the millions who ask principally to go their own way in decency and dignity, and to have their own rights accorded the same respect they accord the rights of others. Only if he listens to the quiet voices can he be true to this trust. . . .

The Presidency has been called an impossible office.

If I thought it were, I would not be seeking it. But its functions have become cluttered, the President's time drained away in trivia, the channels of authority confused.

When questions of human survival may turn on the judgments of one man, he must have time to concentrate on those great decisions that only he can make.

One means of achieving this is by expanding the role of the Vice President—which I will do.

I also plan a re-organized and strengthened Cabinet, and a stronger White House staff than any yet put together.

The people are served not only by a President, but by an Administration, and not only by an Administration, but by a government.

The President's chief function is to lead, not to administer; it is not to oversee every detail, but to put the right people in charge, to provide them with basic guidance and direction, and to let them do the job. As Theodore Roosevelt once put it, "the best executive is the one who has enough sense to pick good men to do what he wants done, and self-restraint enough to keep from meddling with them while they do it."

"Many years ago I concluded that a few hair shirts were part of the mental wardrobe of every man. The President differs only from other men in that he has a more extensive wardrobe."
—Herbert Hoover

RICHARD MILHOUS NIXON
1969–

Whatever else it may be, the Presidency is a hard job. Some men have borne its demands better than others, but the burdens of office can safely be said to have been largely responsible for the death of William Henry Harrison a month after he became President and that of James Knox Polk three months after his retirement, and the illnesses of Presidents Wilson and Eisenhower, for other examples. Below, Martin Van Buren comments on the way it feels to be President.

. . . I must not be understood . . . as undervaluing the honor, dignity and usefulness of the Presidential office. No American citizen can fail to regard that position as, in every respect, the most exalted as it is the most responsible public trust that can be conferred. . . . But the extent to which personal happiness and enjoyment will be promoted by its possession is a question to be solved by the taste and temperament of the incumbent. There are men, and not a few, who derive so much pleasure from the mere possession of great power that any degree of dissatisfaction caused by its exercise is not too dear a price for the coveted indulgence, and the personal adulation which is sure to follow the footsteps of authority while it lasts fills the measure of their satisfaction. Those better regulated minds, however, whose gratification on reaching that high office is mainly derived from the consciousness that their countrymen have deemed them worthy of it and from the hope that they may be able to justify that confidence and to discharge its duties so as to promote the public good, will save themselves from great disappointments by postponing all thoughts of individual enjoyment to the completion of their labors. . . .

At the very head of their disappointments will stand those inseparable from the distribution of patronage, that power so dazzling to the expectant dispenser, apparently so easily performed and so fruitful of reciprocal gratification. Whatever hopes they may indulge that their cases will prove an exception to the general rule they will find, in the end, their own experience truly described by Mr. Jefferson when he said that the two happiest days of his life were those of his entrance upon his office and of his surrender of it. The truth of the matter may be stated in a word: whilst to have been deemed worthy by a majority of the People of the United States to fill the office of Chief Magistrate of the Republic is an honor which ought to satisfy the aspirations of the most ambitious citizen, the period of his actual possession of its powers and performance of its duties is and must, from the nature of things, always be, to a right minded man one of toilsome and anxious probation. . . .

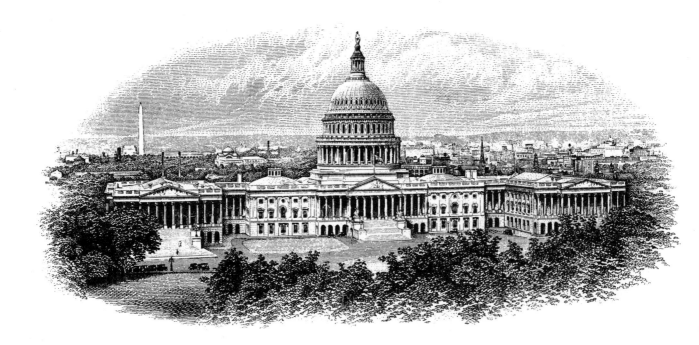

Committees and Events, 1969

The Inaugural Committee particularly wishes to extend its appreciation and thanks to the many other volunteers whose names do not appear below but who gave so generously of their time and services throughout the inaugural.

OFFICE OF EXECUTIVE DIRECTOR

Robert G. McCune, Executive Director
Jane Pierpoint, Executive Secretary to the Director
I. Marie Smith, Secretary
Lt. Steve S. Clarey, Military Aide to Executive
  Director
Herbert C. Blunck, Special Assistant
Gary A. Terry, Special Assistant
George L. Hooper, Administrative Assistant
Edward R. Fickenscher, Committee Coordinator
  Liaison
Fred L. Dixon, Committee Coordinator
Ernest J. Eaton, Assistant to Coordinator
James B. Morrison, Committee Coordinator
Walter S. Johnson, Assistant to Coordinator
John E. Nidecker, Committee Coordinator
A. J. Nuthall, Committee Coordinator
James A. Rose, Jr., Committee Coordinator
William M. Werber, Committee Coordinator
Barbara Butler, Secretary
Edward D. French, Public Sales Coordinator
Ella Bransom, Assistant
Marge Fox, Assistant
E. Del Smith, Special Sales Coordinator
Gail A. Hemstreet, Secretary
Robert S. Carter, Special Projects Coordinator
John R. MacKenzie, Special Projects Coordinator
E. Christian Stengel, Special Projects Coordinator
Kenneth C. Rietz, Assistant
Peggy J. Barker, Secretary
James E. Bacon, Policy Procurement Coordinator
John A. Donahue, Policy Procurement Coordinator
Grace D. Sisson, Assistant Coordinator
Barbara D. Beverly, Secretary
Dale C. O'Brien, Executive Receptionist
Cyril Clarke, Office Aide

Faith W. Kauders, Secretary
Roger S. Jackson
Maryann Ferko, Secretary
Victor S. Kamber, Director of Administration
Patricia Jean Requa, Administrative Assistant
Judy B. Armstrong, Secretary
Bruce J. Brennan, Special Project Assistant

CENTRAL CORRESPONDENCE SYSTEM

H. Ed Munden, Director
Edna M. Jones, Assistant Director
James C. Barr, Assistant
Franklin W. Roskelley, Mail Room Director
Nicholas A. Lotito, U.S. Post Office Representative
Eunice M. Benjamin, Messenger
Josephine Creighton, Secretary
Jeannette M. Caskie
Dana M. DeMartino
Peggy A. Papp
J. Frederick Sinclair
Carol A. Webster
Timothy T. West

COMMUNICATIONS

Marie A. Snellings, Supervisor
Mary L. Robey, Staff Directory Coordinator
Helen E. Gray, Locator
Sara E. Warner, Locator

GENERAL SERVICES

Fred Radewagen, Office Manager
D. Michael Fisher, Assistant Office Manager
Tana K. Lorenzen, Secretary

INFORMATION CENTER

Maryann Benes, Receptionist
Janet E. O'Donnell, Receptionist

INVITATION CONTROL

Frank E. Wall, Jr., Chairman
Lawrence F. Haug, Jr., Production Supervisor
J. Edgar Nichols, Supervisor
Edgar G. E. Morgan, Supervisor
W. Stanley Armstrong, Supervisor
Anita B. Glover, Supervisor
Karen D. Rietz, Executive Secretary
Marilyn Sherman, Secretary
Ann E. Foster, Secretary
Timothy J. Haug, Messenger
David Miller, Messenger
Mazelle M. Barnes
Robert A. Bradley
Martin Luther Jackson
Fred H. Lippucci
George Pivot
Catherine R. Rietz
Arthur H. Walker

LICENSE PLATE SALES

F. Patrick Butler, Director
P. Suanne Brooks
Betty Cameron
Marjorie E. Cernansky
Alexis A. Goodarzi
Jackie W. Gurkin
Bunny T. Hershenshon
Herman K. Intemann

CONTINUED

Mr. Jefferson Peyser and Mrs. Stanley Lieber, both of San Francisco, Cal.

Mrs. Doray Saddler of Denver, Col.; Mr. and Mrs. Burton F. Wiand of New York City.

Mr. and Mrs. Walter Beran of Cleveland, Ohio.

Mr. and Mrs. Pieter van Beek of Chicago, Illinois.

At the Ball

Rep. Donald E. Lukens of Middletown, Ohio, and Miss June Leonard.

Senator B. Everett Jordan of North Carolina and his daughter, Mrs. Rose Ann Gant.

From left, above, are Mr. and Mrs. J. Willard Marriott, President and Mrs. Nixon, Mr. and Mrs. Mark Evans.

Rep. and Mrs. Donald G. Brotzman of Boulder, Col.

Rep. and Mrs. Robert B. Mathias of Bakersfield, Cal.

Robert C. James
Julie Johnson
James P. Low
Susan J. MacMackin
Alan M. May
Jack B. McDonald
Alice E. Nelson
Frederick J. Oeltjen
Vernon W. Palmer, II
Elvira Robbins
Elizabeth L. Roberts
Sara Shriner
Malvin D. Steinback, Jr.
June A. Thomas

PRINTING AND REPRODUCTION

Edward F. Peete, Printing Supervisor
Mary Barbee
Irvin Cook
James Miller

SECURITY

Paul Fairbank, Director

SUPPLIES AND EQUIPMENT

Martha J. Hill

TELEPHONE SERVICES

Ellis Adams
Bob Burgess
Mike Roney
Betty Williams

MANAGEMENT CONSULTANTS

Dudley P. Kircher
Harry L. Vincent

ARMED FORCES PARTICIPATION COMMITTEE

Maj. Gen. Charles S. O'Malley, Jr. USA, Chairman
Rear Adm. Donald G. Irvine, USN
Rear Adm. Roderick Y. Edwards, USCG
Maj. Gen. Nils O. Ohman, USAF
Col. F. L. Franzman, USMC

JOINT EXECUTIVE COMMITTEE

Col. R. C. Hamilton, USA, Chairman
Col. F. L. Franzman, USMC
Capt. W. L. Garrett, Jr., USN
Col. Wirt Corrie, USAF
Cdr. Terrence McDonald, USCG
Lt. Frederick B. Heck, USAF, Special Assistant
Lt. Andrew J. Zusi, USMC, Special Assistant

SECRETARIAT

Maj. Henry J. Touhey, USA
1st Lt. Ruth D. Walsh, USMC
Miss Linda Kriebel
Lt. Col. Donald E. Honeman, USA, Liaison to
  Chairman

PARADE SUBCOMMITTEE

Lt. Col. Paul C. Miller, USA (Ret), Chairman
Mrs. Ann Duckworth
M.Sgt. John M. Carroll, USA
Sgt. Andrew S. Wood, USA
SP4 Clara E. Steves, USA
Lt. Col. Edward D. Bennett, USMC
Mr. H. A. Friedenberg, USCG
Lt. Col. Robert A. Smoak, USAF
Lt. Cdr. John R. Lawson, USN
Lt. Michael Impellizzeri, USA
Maj. E. K. Schroeder, USA
Lt. Cdr. R. E. Lauk, USN
Lt. (jg) A. L. Myers, USN
Lt. Col. W. H. Disher, USMC
Lt. Col. Harold Coplan, USAF
Lt. Col. Melvin Johnson, USAF
Maj. Robert L. Davenport, USA
Maj. L. R. Gaboury, USMC
Lt. Cdr. John O. Richter, Jr., USN
Maj. Jack Beall, USAF
Lt. Cdr. D. R. Casey, USCG
Col. W. J. Bates, USA
Maj. Thomas King, USAF
Lt. Col. Samuel R. Loboda, USA
M.Sgt. Howard Pond, USA
Lt. Col. Robert Stuart, USAF
Capt. Thomas E. Moritz, USAF
Col. L. B. Carter, USA
Capt. Philip J. Murphy, USMC

1st Lt. James R. Proudfit, USMC

PUBLIC INFORMATION SUBCOMMITTEE

Col. L. H. Sims, Jr., USA, Chairman
Capt. D. L. Hanson, USA
Cdr. J. D. Dawson, USN
Capt. William H. Cobb, USAF
Lt. Cdr. J. W. Duenzl, USCG
1st Lt. Harold S. Gazaway, USMC

MILITARY AIDES SUBCOMMITTEE

Lt. Col. Marc A. Moore, USMC, Chairman
Lt. Col. Robert C. Keller, USAF
Cdr. Alden B. Anderson, USN
Cdr. John C. Fuechsel, USCG
Maj. George J. Raunam, USA
YNC Guy A. Brace, USN
YN2 Jerome P. Evanosky, USCG
Cpl. Terry V. Kluender, USMC
SP4 Thomas C. Adler, USA

MILITARY AIDES—ARMY

Lt. Col. Thurman E. Anderson
Lt. Col. Willis G. Bacon
Lt. Col. Frank H. Baker
Lt. Col. Robert E. Butler
Lt. Col. James R. Cook
Lt. Col. Dan L. Crury
Lt. Col. George R. Dawson
Lt. Col. William I. Fox
Lt. Col. Clarance D. Gilkey
Lt. Col. Joseph R. Gilmore
Lt. Col. Thomas F. Healy
Lt. Col. Franklin D. Hicks
Lt. Col. Robert C. Hock
Lt. Col. Glenn S. Meader
Lt. Col. Linsey B. Minturn
Lt. Col. Charles W. Mooney
Lt. Col. Donald J. Pagel
Lt. Col. Frederick R. Pole
Lt. Col. Harley E. Rice
Lt. Col. Marvin Rosenstein
Lt. Col. Gerald E. Royals
Lt. Col. Edward Schowalter
Lt. Col. Grayson D. Tate, Jr.
Lt. Col. Jules C. Trepagnier, Jr.
Lt. Col. Robert D. Vaughn
Lt. Col. Frank G. Walton
Lt. Col. George K. Withers
Lt. Col. John W. Young
Lt. Col. Thomas C. Young
Maj. Harold R. Archibald
Maj. Paul C. Bayruns
Maj. Stephen V. Boylan
Maj. Glenn L. Bruskiewicz
Maj. Kenneth E. Cook
Maj. Philip W. DiMauro
Maj. Quiton A. Freeman
Maj. Leayle G. Galiber
Maj. Paul J. Gorey
Maj. Stephan R. Pawlik
Maj. Joyce S. Perlow
Maj. Glen W. Pohly
Maj. Thurman D. Rodgers
Maj. Ted G. Westerman

MILITARY AIDES—NAVY

Cdr. Thomas A. Boyce
Cdr. Peter C. Conrad
Cdr. Edward C. Copeland
Cdr. Paul H. Engel
Cdr. Richard V. Fox
Cdr. Paul T. Gillchrist
Cdr. Estel W. Hays
Cdr. Richard B. Howe
Cdr. Kenneth P. Hughes
Cdr. Arthur P. Ismay
Cdr. James F. Jenista
Cdr. Frederic H. M. Kinley
Cdr. John R. Kint
Cdr. Arthur M. Osbourne
Cdr. Charles P. Phleger
Cdr. Russell A. Preble
Cdr. Jerome Rapkin
Cdr. Raymond E. Reffitt
Cdr. Joseph C. Smith
Cdr. Lewis B. Sykes
Cdr. D. Bruce Wile
Lt. Cdr. Makoto Araki
Lt. Cdr. Lee N. Brown
Lt. Cdr. Edgar G. Bullock
Lt. Cdr. Thomas G. Campbell
Lt. Cdr. Jefferson R. Dennis, Jr.
Lt. Cdr. Harry M. S. Gimber
Lt. Cdr. Irving K. Goto

Lt. Cdr. Thomas P. James, Jr.
Lt. Cdr. John M. Leaver
Lt. Cdr. Gilbert R. Mesec
Lt. Cdr. Charles F. Noll
Lt. Cdr. Edward G. Ogden
Lt. Cdr. Velmer A. J. Winn
Lt. Janice L. Heidt
Lt. Hillar Sarepera

MILITARY AIDES—MARINE CORPS

Col. Robert L. Shufford
Lt. Col. Vincente T. Blaz
Lt. Col. Donald K. Cliff
Lt. Col. John Colia
Lt. Col. Marcus J. Gravel
Lt. Col. Andrew E. Hare
Lt. Col. Frederick S. Johnson
Lt. Col. Earl H. Lillestrand
Lt. Col. Jack L. Reed
Lt. Col. Robert R. Sheahan
Lt. Col. William H. Thousand
Lt. Col. John L. Zorack
Maj. James J. Chmelik
Maj. George E. Gaumont
Maj. Adele A. Graham
Maj. John H. Havel
Maj. Richard F. Johnson
Maj. Wilbur C. McMinn
Maj. Antonio Mediavilla
Maj. Thomas P. Miller
Maj. Michael F. Welty

MILITARY AIDES—AIR FORCE

Col. Douglas J. McGill
Lt. Col. Charles E. Akard
Lt. Col. Eli L. Beeding, Jr.
Lt. Col. Samuel H. Bohinc
Lt. Col. Henry A. Collin, Jr.
Lt. Col. John L. Covey
Lt. Col. David F. Crawford
Lt. Col. Roy L. DeHart
Lt. Col. Ole P. Flaa
Lt. Col. David S. Kahne
Lt. Col. Donald A. Loren
Lt. Col. Lloyd F. Meyer
Lt. Col. Michael M. Mitchell
Lt. Col. Thomas A. Olson
Lt. Col. Phillip R. Shepherd
Lt. Col. Thaddeus S. Skladzien
Lt. Col. Jerald H. Thompson
Lt. Col. George N. Watkins
Maj. Blake B. Allred
Maj. Wallace S. Berg
Maj. Wayne L. Christison
Maj. George F. Dempsey
Maj. Calvin J. Frazier
Maj. Frank D. Hills
Maj. Lawrence A. Keefe
Maj. Romain F. Krzmarzick
Maj. Richard H. Lally
Maj. Leslie D. Nordhaugen
Maj. Arden B. Pepper, Jr.
Maj. Roger A. Scott
Maj. Edward E. Skipper
Maj. Leslie C. Slaybaugh
Maj. Robert J. Smith
Maj. George N. Winkler
Capt. Audrey J. Page

MILITARY AIDES—COAST GUARD

Cdr. Charles A. Biondo
Cdr. William B. Clark
Cdr. Clifford F. DeWolf
Cdr. Thomas F. Hawkins
Cdr. James C. Irwin
Cdr. H. H. Kothe
Cdr. Edward N. Nelson, Jr.
Cdr. Hal F. Olson
Cdr. Richard T. Penn
Cdr. Clyde E. Robbins
Cdr. Claude R. Thompson
Cdr. Albert C. Tingley
Cdr. Norman C. Venzke
Lt. Cdr. Gilbert E. Brown
Lt. Cdr. Stephen J. Dasovich
Lt. Cdr. Ralph W. Eustis
Lt. Cdr. Terrence J. Montonye
Lt. Cdr. John F. Otranto, Jr.
Lt. Cdr. William F. Roland
Lt. Cdr. Peter J. Rots
Lt. Cdr. Brinton R. Shannon

LOGISTICS SUBCOMMITTEE

Col. J. H. Brown, USA, Chairman
Lt. Col. C. H. Kemp, USA
Lt. Col. Thomas G. Foster, USAF

Lt. Col. Ullie C. Wells, USMC
Lt. Cdr. C. H. Hergesheimer, USN
Lt. Cdr. J. H. Hedgecock, USCG

TRANSPORTATION SUBCOMMITTEE

Cdr. C. Courtright, USN, Chairman
1st Lt. Frank N. Green, USMC
Maj. Robert L. Nichols, USAF
Lt. Cdr. K. R. Murphy, USCG
Mr. E. M. Townshend, USA
Mr. Charles M. Wicks, USN

SPECIAL EVENTS SUBCOMMITTEE

Col. Herbert Rosenthal, USAF, Chairman
Lt. Cdr. P. F. Bodling, Jr., USN
Maj. Herbert L. Seay, USMC
Lt. Col. L. F. Boring, USA
Cdr. R. H. Wood, USCG

MEDICAL SUBCOMMITTEE

Col. O. W. Snyder, USA, Chairman
Maj. W. O. Davis, USA
Lt. Cdr. R. L. Wentworth, USN
Lt. Col. Nickolas F. Kobylk, USAF
Capt. Ralph K. Neff, USAF
Mr. Martin Ruebens, USCG

BUDGET COMMITTEE

W. Leslie Douglas, Chairman
Webb C. Hayes III, Co-Chairman
Buford Scott
George L. Dixon
Richard Egbert
Robert Dudley
William R. Bush
Temple Seay
Johnathan Sloat
Cornelius Shields, Jr.

CIVIC PARTICIPATION COMMITTEE

William H. Press, Chairman
Mrs. Margaret Haywood, Vice Chairman
William A. Ulman, Executive Vice Chairman
Mrs. Josephine M. Maddox, Secretary and
  Clerk-Aide
Robert C. Heina, Administrative Assistant

SUBCOMMITTEE CHAIRMEN

Thomas E. Boyce, Professional
Richmond M. Keeney, Local Governments
William K. Norwood, Citizens Assns.
Hugh N. Phillips, Service Clubs
Robert L. Tull, Business
J. C. Turner, Labor Unions

HONORARY MEMBERS

Mr. and Mrs. Floyd Anderson
Mrs. Vivian Ashton
Lewis T. Breuninger, Sr.
B. Bernei Burgunder, Jr.
Mr. and Mrs. Enoch Butler
Mrs. Claude Cowan
Edmund W. Dreyfuss
Mr. and Mrs. Samuel Friday, Jr.
Clyde D. Garrett
Mrs. Ethel Grubbs
Mrs. Marian H. Jackson
Mrs. Laurice Juggins
J. Paul Marshall
Jack Mills
William C. Mott
Mr. and Mrs. Alonzo Mundy
John A. Nevius
Robert L. O'Brien, Jr.
Mrs. Marie M. Rogers
James B. Ward

CONCERT COMMITTEE

Mrs. Marjorie Merriweather Post,
  Honorary Chairman
Dr. S. Dillon Ripley, II, Chairman
Mrs. Carl L. Shipley, Co-Chairman
M. Robert Rogers, Executive Director
Jesse R. Smith, Choir Coordinator
Malise C. Bloch, Staff Coordinator
Mrs. Elliott Dodd Degraff, Invitations Director
Charles L. Clapp, Assistant to the Secretary,
  Smithsonian Institution
Mrs. Robert Low Bacon
Robert C. Baker
Hon. Frances Bolton
Mrs. Edward Brooke, Sr.

Hon. Ralph Bunche
Mrs. Benjamin Evans, Jr.
Hon. Luis Ferre
Mrs. John Clifford Folger
Mrs. George Garrett
Mrs. Philip Graham
Melville B. Grosvenor
Hon. Gordon Gray
George Hamilton, Jr.
L. A. Jennings
Samuel Kauffman
Donald M. Kendall
Milton King
Mrs. Charles Hamilton Maddox
Mrs. John McCone
Mrs. Robert McCormick
Hon. L. Quincy Mumford
Mrs. Jouett Shouse
Mrs. Jessie Snowden
Hobart Spalding
Hon. Roger Stevens
Lloyd Symington
John Walker
Hon. Walter Washington
Osby Weir

CONCESSIONS COMMITTEE

EXECUTIVE COMMITTEE

Berkeley G. Burrell, Chairman
Robert E. McLaughlin, Vice Chairman
Iverson O. Mitchell, Deputy Chairman
William R. Evans, Executive Director
Rita M. Smith, Administrative Assistant

SUBCOMMITTEE CHAIRMEN

Mary Gardiner Jones, Souvenir Review
Hudson Moses, Location & Construction Stands
Arminger Jagoe, Insurance
Mrs. Jean Sisco, Sales Promotion

COMMITTEE MEMBERS

Robert N. Beck
Fred M. Downey
Dr. Malcolm C. Hope
O. F. Maltagliati
Leland S. McCarthy
C. Francis Murphy
Daniel H. Osborne
Robert C. Peck
George O. Pierce
Theodore Smith
Aubrey C. Woodard
Dr. Murray Grant
Val Washington
Mrs. Lillian V. Engelstad
Mrs. Norma Rogers

CONGRESSIONAL LIAISON COMMITTEE

Douglas Whitlock, Chairman
Richard S. Tribbe, Vice Chairman
Wayne W. Bradley
Hugh C. Cannon
R. Daniel Devlin
Mrs. Irene Fistere
Harold Forsythe
Mrs. Helen Hock
Jerome Hoobler
Mrs. Kate Johnston
Miss Joy Langford
Bruce F. Merkle
Field Reichardt
Robert E. Ruddy
Delbert O. Johnson
Cpl. Roger Jones

DECORATIONS COMMITTEE

Leon Chatelain, Jr., Chairman
Vlastimil Koubek, Vice Chairman
James P. Callmer
Theo. J. Christensen
Theodore W. Dominick
H. Thomas Driver
Walter L. Jubien
James Morrison
Robert J. Nash
George W. Petticord, Jr.
Richard E. Steen
Charles M. Stover
Boris Timchenko

DISTINGUISHED LADIES RECEPTION

Mrs. Dwight D. Eisenhower, Honorary Chairman

Mrs. J. Willard Marriott, Chairman
Mrs. C. Wayland Brooks, Co-Chairman
Mrs. Ray Bliss, Honorary Vice Chairman
Mme. Julia Grant Canacuzene, Honorary
  Vice Chairman
Mrs. John Foster Dulles, Honorary Vice Chairman
Mrs. Christian Herter, Honorary Vice Chairman
Mrs. Patricia Reilly Hitt, Honorary Vice Chairman
Mrs. Howard Jenkins, Jr., Honorary Vice Chairman
Mrs. Nicholas Longworth, Honorary Vice Chairman
Mrs. Gladys O'Donnell, Honorary Vice Chairman
Mrs. William P. Rogers, Honorary Vice Chairman
Mrs. Mary Jane McCaffree, Executive
  Vice Chairman
Mrs. Lawson McKenzie, Coordinator
Mrs. M. Williams Blake, Coordinator
Mrs. Roy E. James, Coordinator
Mrs. Everett Dirksen, Chairman, U.S. Senate Wives
Mrs. Gerald Ford, Chairman, U.S. House of
  Representatives Wives
Mrs. Whitney Gillilland, Chairman, Official
  Inauguration Hostesses
Mrs. Perkins McGuire, Co-Chairman, Diplomatic
  Hostesses
Mrs. Douglas Weaver, Co-Chairman, Diplomatic
  Hostesses
Mrs. Benjamin C. Evans, Co-Chairman, Junior
  Inauguration Hostesses
Mrs. Robert E. Long, Co-Chairman, Junior
  Inauguration Hostesses

CONGRESSIONAL HOSTESSES

Mrs. E. Ross Adair
Mrs. George D. Aiken
Mrs. Gordon Allott
Mrs. John B. Anderson
Mrs. Mark Andrews
Mrs. William H. Ayres
Mrs. Howard H. Baker, Jr.
Mrs. William H. Bates
Mrs. James F. Battin
Mrs. Page Belcher
Mrs. Wallace F. Bennett
Mrs. Jackson E. Betts
Mrs. Edward W. Brooke
Mrs. Frank T. Bow
Mrs. W. E. Brock III
Mrs. William S. Broomfield
Mrs. Donald G. Brotzman
Mrs. Clarence J. Brown, Jr.
Mrs. James T. Broyhill
Mrs. Joel T. Broyhill
Mrs. John Hall Buchanan
Mrs. Lawrence J. Burton
Mrs. George Bush
Mrs. John W. Byrnes
Mrs. Clifford P. Case
Mrs. Elford A. Cederberg
Mrs. Charles E. Chamberlain
Mrs. Barber B. Conable
Mrs. Silvio O. Conte
Mrs. Marlow W. Cook
Mrs. John Sherman Cooper
Mrs. Robert J. Corbett
Mrs. William C. Cramer
Mrs. Carl T. Curtis
Mrs. Glen R. Davis
Mrs. John R. Dellenback
Mrs. Robert V. Denney
Mrs. Edward J. Derwinski
Mrs. Samuel L. Devine
Mrs. Robert Dole
Mrs. Peter H. Dominick
Hon. Florence P. Dwyer
Mrs. Jack Edwards
Mrs. Marvin L. Esch
Mrs. Paul J. Fannin
Mrs. Peter H. B. Frelinghuysen
Mrs. Charles E. Goodell
Mrs. H. R. Gross
Mrs. Gilbert Gude
Mrs. Durward G. Hall
Mrs. Clifford P. Hansen
Mrs. George V. Hansen
Mrs. William H. Harsha
Mrs. James Harvey
Mrs. Craig Hosmer
Mrs. Roman L. Hruska
Mrs. Edward Hutchinson
Mrs. Charles Raper Jonas, Sr.
Mrs. Hastings Keith
Mrs. Thomas S. Kleppe
Mrs. Dan H. Kuykendall
Mrs. Odin Langen
Mrs. Glenard P. Lipscomb
Mrs. James McClure
Mrs. William M. McCulloch

CONTINUED

Reception for Distinguished Ladies

The Reception for Distinguished Ladies was held January 18—the Saturday before the inauguration—at the National Gallery of Art. Among the guests were women who have made their mark in the arts and in public service, the wives of government officials, and the wives of foreign diplomats. At left, with Mrs. Nixon: Mrs. Aoua Keita, wife of the Mali ambassador, and Mrs. Gallin-

Douathe, wife of the ambassador of the Central African Republic. Mrs. Nixon shared the pleasant duties of the receiving line with, among others: in the top left picture, Mrs. Robert Finch, Mrs. Hugh Scott, Mrs. Strom Thurmond; at top right, Mrs. Eisenhower, Mrs. Winton Blount, Mrs. Everett M. Dirksen; at bottom left, Mrs. David Kennedy and Mrs. J. Willard Marriott.

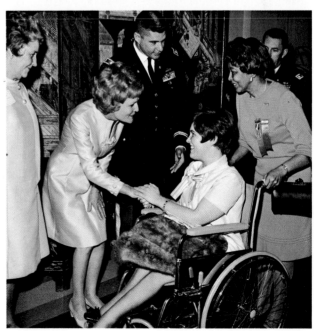

Mrs. Clark MacGregor
Mrs. William S. Mailliard
Mrs. Robert B. Mathias
Hon. Catherine May
Mrs. Wiley Mayne
Mrs. William E. Minshall
Mrs. Chester L. Mize
Mrs. Alvin E. O'Konski
Mrs. Thomas M. Pelly
Mrs. Charles H. Percy
Mrs. Jerry L. Pettis
Mrs. Richard H. Poff
Mrs. Albert H. Quie
Mrs. Thomas F. Railsback
Hon. Charlotte T. Reid
Mrs. Ogden R. Reid
Mrs. Ben Reifel
Mrs. John J. Rhodes
Mrs. Donald W. Riegle, Jr.
Mrs. Howard W. Robison
Mrs. Donald Rumsfeld
Mrs. Herman T. Schneebeli
Mrs. Garner E. Shriver
Mrs. H. Allen Smith
Mrs. Henry P. Smith III
Mrs. James V. Smith
Mrs. William L. Springer
Mrs. Robert T. Stafford
Mrs. J. William Stanton
Mrs. Burt L. Talcott
Mrs. Guy Vander Jagt
Mrs. William C. Wampler
Mrs. William B. Widnall
Mrs. Charles E. Wiggins
Mrs. Robert Wilson
Mrs. Larry Winn, Jr.
Mrs. Louis C. Wyman
Mrs. Roger Zion

DIPLOMATIC HOSTESSES

Mrs. Howard C. Adams
Miss Bertha S. Adkins
Mrs. Floyd Akers
Mrs. Augusto Guillermo Arango
Mrs. Robert K. Beahan
Mrs. Ralph E. Becker
Mrs. George T. Bell
Mrs. Herbert C. Blunck
Mrs. William H. Brett
Mrs. C. K. Browne
Mrs. Percival F. Brundage
Mrs. William F. Burdick
Mrs. W. Randolph Burgess
Mrs. George Burkhardt III
Mrs. Morris Cafritz
Mrs. Leonard Carmichael
Mrs. Claire Lee Chennault
Mrs. Blair Childs
Mrs. David P. Close
Mrs. Mark H. Cornell
Mrs. Arthur Chase Cox
Mrs. Kenneth Crosby
Mrs. William Hooper Dayton
Mrs. J. Hunter Drum
Mrs. Julian Dugas
Mrs. Allen W. Dulles
Mrs. Marcella Miller duPont
Mrs. John S. D. Eisenhower
Mrs. Dorothy Elston
Mrs. Mark Evans
Miss Meta Morris Evans
Mrs. Austin Fickling
Mrs. Robert W. Fleming
Mrs. John Clifford Folger
Mrs. George M. Fuller
Mrs. Arthur Gardner
Mrs. George A. Garrett
Mrs. Whitney Gilliland
Mrs. Hyde Gillette
Mrs. C. Leslie Glenn
Hon. Louise Gore
Mrs. J. R. Gorman
Mrs. Gilbert Hahn, Jr.
Mrs. Kay Hanson
Mrs. George L. Hart, Jr.
Mrs. Paul H. Hatch
Mrs. Webb C. Hayes III
Mrs. A. B. Hermann
Mrs. James M. Johnston
Mrs. Samuel H. Kauffmann
Mrs. John Morrison Kerr
Mrs. McCook Knox
Mrs. Robert Le Baron
Mrs. James H. Lemon, Sr.
Lady Lewis
Mrs. William P. MacCracken
Mrs. Russell Marriott
Mrs. I. Jack Martin
Mrs. William Beverley Mason, Jr.

Mrs. Robert R. McCormick
Mrs. Joseph C. McGarraghy
Mrs. Grayson McGuire
Mrs. Donald McPherson
Mrs. Howard Mitchell
Mrs. George Gordon Moore
Mrs. Jerry Moore
Mrs. Logan Morris
Mrs. Loren K. Olson
Mrs. Tompkins Parker
Mrs. Merriweather Post
Mrs. Warren Price, Jr.
Mrs. Elwood R. Quesada
Mrs. Arthur W. Radford
Mrs. Charles S. Rhyne
Mrs. Eugene H. Rietzke
Mrs. Roy St. Lewis
Mrs. Kurt Salmon
Mrs. Carl L. Shipley
Mrs. Richard Simpson
Mrs. Lewis Strauss
Mrs. A. Burke Summers
Mrs. J. Laning Taylor
Mrs. J. Mark Trice
Mrs. Leigh Wade
Mrs. Wesley Williams
Mrs. James Wimsatt
Mrs. Paul Zahl
Mrs. Rose Saul Zalles

OFFICIAL INAUGURAL HOSTESSES

Mrs. Muriel Alexander
Mrs. Robert Amory
Mrs. J. Breckinridge Bayne
Mrs. Samuel Botts
Mrs. Parke Brady
Mrs. Ella Mae Bransom
Mrs. Edward Brooke, Sr.
Mrs. George Bunker
Mrs. Robert Campbell
Mrs. Harry Tyson Carter
Mrs. John C. Chapin
Mrs. Robert M. Clark
Mrs. William C. Coe
Mrs. Raymond E. Cox
Mrs. William Smith Culbertson
Mrs. Frederick J. Cullen
Mrs. Neil Dietrich
Mrs. Henry T. Donaldson
Mrs. Russell Dorr
Mrs. Peter Du Bose
Mrs. Harold D. Fangboner
Mrs. Homer Ferguson
Mrs. Alfred Goldstein
Mrs. Cecil G. Grant
Mrs. George E. C. Hayes
Mrs. Margaret A. Haywood
Mrs. Norman Jarvis
Mrs. Howard Jenkins, Jr.
Mrs. George Kronmiller
Mrs. Woodrow Marriott
Mrs. Willie Mason
Mrs. Katherine B. Massenburg
Mrs. Gladys T. Montgomery
Mrs. Virginia Morris
Mrs. Cynthia S. Newman
Mrs. Mandell J. Ourisman
Mrs. Barrington D. Parker
Mrs. Henry S. Robinson
Mrs. Andreas Ronhovde
Mrs. Louis Rothschild
Mrs. William S. Thompson
Mrs. Richard H. Todd
Mrs. Sterling Tucker
Mrs. C. Langhorne Washburn
Mrs. Val Washington
Mrs. Edward I. Williams, Jr.

JUNIOR HOSTESSES

Mrs. Steven Adair
Mrs. Dorrance Belin
Miss Gail Bellmon
Miss Pat Bellmon
Mrs. Henry A. Berliner
Mrs. Raymond C. Brophy
Miss Shirley Browne
Mrs. Mel Burton
Miss Bonnie Byrnes
Miss Michelle Conte
Miss Sylvia Conte
Mrs. Jerry Cunningham
Mrs. Edward Curran
Miss Carol Devine
Miss Joyce Devine
Mrs. Benjamin C. Evans, Jr.
Mrs. Lee M. Folger
Miss Ann Foster

Mrs. Randolph A. Frank
Miss Beatrice Frelinghuysen
Mrs. Charles E. Galloway
Miss Jayne Gillenwaters
Mrs. Peter L. Gilsey
Mrs. Richard B. Griffin, Jr.
Mrs. Gilbert M. Grosvenor
Miss Diane Harvey
Mrs. John Hedden
Mrs. William H. Hessick III
Mrs. Scott Heuer, Jr.
Miss Susan Hosmer
Miss Jana Hruska
Miss Karel Huffman
Mrs. Norma F. Hurley
Mrs. James F. C. Hyde, Jr.
Mrs. Russell E. Iler
Mrs. George D. Iverson
Mrs. Charles R. Jonas
Mrs. William R. Joyce, Jr.
Mrs. Robert E. Long
Miss Nancy McCulloch
Mrs. J. W. Marriott, Jr.
Mrs. Richard E. Marriott
Miss Judy Martin
Mrs. Charles T. Matheson
Miss Melinda May
Mrs. J. M. Mitchell, Jr.
Mrs. Ted Newman
Mrs. Patrick O'Donnell
Mrs. S. Parker Oliphant
Mrs. Raymond K. Poole
Mrs. Richard Powell
Miss Marta Schneebeli
Mrs. Paul E. Shorb, Jr.
Miss Lucinda B. Smith
Miss Katherine Springer
Mrs. Tillman Stirling
Miss Joyce Streeter
Mrs. William B. Ward
Mrs. Fran Westner
Mrs. Henry K. Willard II
Miss Cindy Winn
Miss Felicity Yost
Mrs. David Zimmers

EXECUTIVE HOSTESSES

Miss Barbara Burns
Mrs. Isabel M. Cek
Miss Esther H. Esmond
Miss Frances Griffin
Mrs. Florence Harrill
Miss Barbara Johnston
Miss Betty Lantz
Miss Ruth Manchester
Mrs. Leonard R. Raish
Mrs. Clara Row
Mrs. Felix Sklagen
Mrs. Barbara Sweeney
Miss Carol Windram

FINANCE COMMITTEE

Robert C. Baker, Chairman
George Olmsted, Vice Chairman
Barnum L. Colton, Vice Chairman
L. A. Jennings, Treasurer
Henry K. Willard II, Assistant to the Chairman

EXECUTIVE COMMITTEE

Floyd D. Akers
George M. Bunker
Edward Burling, Jr.
Kenneth M. Crosby
William L. Lindholm
C. J. Mack
George Meany
J. William Middendorf II
Andrew H. Parker
Rudolph A. Peterson
Gustave Ring
William G. Whyte

COMMITTEE MEMBERS

James W. Aston
Dominic Antonelli
Edward C. Baltz
Joseph A. Beirne
Willard O. Bent
Leo M. Bernstein
William R. Biggs
Donald S. Bittinger
Herbert C. Blunck
Crosby N. Boyd
Howard Boyd
W. A. Boyle
R. Manning Brown, Jr.

George S. Burrus
Calvin Cafritz
Leon Chatelain, Jr.
William Calomiris
E. Taylor Chewning
Robert M. Clark
Sylvan C. Coleman
John F. Connelly
Marshall B. Coyne
Lorimer A. Davidson
F. Elwood Davis
George W. DeFranceaux
Leonard B. Doggett, Jr.
John B. Duncan
R. Roy Dunn
Dr. Milton L. Elsberg
William H. G. Fitzgerald
Edward H. Foley
James Franklin
Robert H. Gerdes
Thomas M. Goodfellow
Albert H. Gordon
Robert L. Gordon, Jr.
Philip L. Gore
Kingdon Gould, Jr.
Frank A. Gunther
Randall H. Hagner, Jr.
L. P. Harrell
Dr. Milton I. Harris
Nelson T. Hartson
Lloyd Holroyd
Frank N. Ikard
Vernon A. Johnson
Edward K. Jones
Howard W. Kacy
Garfield I. Kass
W. John Kenney
Dan A. Kimball
William T. Leith
Moe Lerner
J. Willard Marriott, Jr.
Robert M. McElwaine
T. P. McLachlen
Harry L. Merrick, Sr.
Charles F. Meyers, Jr.
John W. Miller
Don Mitchell
B. Doyle Mitchell
Col. G. Gordon Moore
Dr. James M. Nabritt
Richard A. Norris
A. Chambers Oliphant
Thornton W. Owen
Louis C. Paladini
Barrington D. Parker
Donald J. Parsons
Mrs. Merriweather Post
Gen. Elwood H. Quesada
Richard S. Reynolds
William J. Schuiling
Edward H. Selonick
William E. Shannon
J. Robert Sherwood
Carlton D. Smith
Charles Emil Smith
Douglas R. Smith
Dale H. Smith
W. Clement Stone
John W. Sweeterman
Dr. Charles Allen Thomas
Jack Valenti
Charls E. Walker
Thomas J. Watson, Jr.
Charles H. Weaver
Sidney J. Weinberg
Osby L. Weir
Dr. Charles Stanley White
William B. Willard
Stephen Woodzell
William C. Yowell

GOVERNORS' RECEPTION COMMITTEE

Maj. Gen. George Olmsted, Chairman
Robert W. Fleming, Co-Chairman
R. Webster Chamberlin, Executive Vice Chairman
Francis W. Crary, Executive Vice Chairman
Lily M. Beauchamp, Special Assistant to Chairman
John E. Horton, Special Advisor to Chairman
Justin D. Bowersock, Treasurer

INVITATIONS SUBCOMMITTEE

I. Lee Potter, Chairman
Mrs. Elmer R. Hipsley, Co-Chairman

PRESS RELATIONS SUBCOMMITTEE

Mrs. Claire L. Chennault, Chairman

Mrs. E. Edward Cavin, Co-Chairman
Mrs. Hope Ridings Miller, Co-Chairman
Fred C. Milner, Co-Chairman

PERSONAL SERVICES SUBCOMMITTEE

Robert D. Ladd, Chairman
J. Louis Smith III, Co-Chairman
Miss Rose R. Blakely, Co-Chairman
Miss Mary Widener, Co-Chairman

MILITARY AIDES SUBCOMMITTEE

Lt. Col. Marc C. Moore, USMC, Chairman

CIVILIAN AIDES SUBCOMMITTEE

George Ferris, Jr., Chairman

SPECIAL PROJECTS SUBCOMMITTEE

Mrs. Joseph Ives, Jr., Chairman

PARKING SUBCOMMITTEE

Bruce Alexander, Chairman

MEDICAL AIDES SUBCOMMITTEE

Dr. William H. Cooper, Chairman

GOVERNORS' LUNCHEON SUBCOMMITTEE

Hon. Leslie Arends, Chairman
Mrs. Claire L. Chennault, Co-Chairman
Mrs. Rose Saul Zalles, Co-Chairman
James N. Juliana, Assistant to Chairman
Mrs. Frank Kilroy, Assistant to Chairman
William Pitts, Assistant to Chairman

RECEPTION ARRANGEMENTS SUBCOMMITTEE

Fred L. Dixon, Chairman

MUSIC SUBCOMMITTEE

Richard Bales, Chairman

PROTOCOL SUBCOMMITTEE

Hon. Clem Conger, Chairman

HOSTESSES SUBCOMMITTEE

Mrs. George D. Aiken, Chairman
Mrs. Perkins McGuire, Co-Chairman
Mrs. Charles Bresler, Co-Chairman
Mrs. Nord Schwiebert, Co-Chairman
Miss Barbara Spillinger, Co-Chairman

SECURITY SUBCOMMITTEE

Adm. Harold Baker, Chairman

FLOOR COMMITTEE SUBCOMMITTEE

J. Hunter Drum, Chairman
Stephen Edwards, Co-Chairman

HOTEL ARRANGEMENTS SUBCOMMITTEE

Nord Schwiebert, Chairman

STAFF

Miss Carole M. Anderson
Mrs. Patricia Foringer
Mrs. Lurlyne B. Martin
Mrs. Jeanne Rush
Mrs. Doris Taylor

HONORARY VICE CHAIRMEN

Hon. Meade Alcorn
Hon. Bertha Adkins
Hon. Tom Baldridge
Ralph E. Becker
Hon. Ezra Taft Benson
Hon. Ray C. Bliss
Fred J. Borch
Lewis T. Breuninger
Hon. John Bricker
Hon. Mary Brooks
Hon. Herbert Brownell, Jr.
Hon. Wiley T. Buchanan, Jr.
Hon. Dean Burch
Sterling Cole
Hon. Thomas E. Dewey

Mrs. C. Douglas Dillon
Hon. Allen Dulles
Mrs. Dorothy Elston
Edward H. Foley
Hon. John Clifford Folger
Hon. Henry H. Fowler
Hon. Guy George Gabrielson
Mrs. O. Max Gardner
Thomas M. Goodfellow
Werner P. Gullander
Hon. Leonard W. Hall
Hon. John D. M. Hamilton
Hon. Goerge L. Hart, Jr.
Hon. George Humphrey
Mrs. Laddie F. Hutar
Howard L. Jenkins
Hon. Walter Judd
Austin H. Kiplinger
Barry T. Leithead
Hon. John V. Lindsay
Mrs. Alice Roosevelt Longworth
John D. Marsh
Hon. Neil McElroy
Hon. Joseph C. McGarraghy
Dale Miller
Hon. William E. Miller
Hon. Gerald D. Morgan
Hon. Thruston Morton
Francis W. Pershing
Lt. Gen. William W. Quinn
Hon. Wesley Robertson
Dr. Henry S. Robinson, Jr.
Hon. Hugh Scott
Hon. William W. Scranton
Hon. Fred Seaton
Mrs. S. Carl Shank
Bernard Shanley
Hon. Robert E. Smylie
Hon. John W. Snyder
Adm. Lewis Strauss
Hon. Arthur Summerfield
Hon. A. Burks Summers
John W. Warner
John C. Whitaker
Charles E. Wilkinson
Mrs. Ellis Yost

COMMITTEE MEMBERS

Cdr. A. B. Anderson, USN
Julian Barber
Mrs. L. Lee Bean, Jr.
Mrs. Ralph E. Becker
Bob Bonitati
Mrs. Nancy Boykins
Mrs. Barbara Boyle
Mrs. Parke H. Brady
Mr. and Mrs. Robert Brinkmeyer
Dale Bruce
Mrs. Arleigh Burke
Miss Barbara Burns
Miss Lynda Clancy
Earl Cocke
Eugene S. Cowen
Miss Connie Crigler
Mrs. William Crouch
Miss Pamela Curtis
Frank DeMarco
Miss Glenna DeQuoy
William L. Devries
Joseph Deweese
Mrs. J. Hunter Drum
Dale Duvall
Mr. and Mrs. Don Duvall
Mrs. J. Lee Estridge
Mrs. George Fuller
Mrs. Hyde Gillette
Mrs. Whitney Gillilland
Phil Guarino
B. H. Hill
Miss Jana Hruska
Ed Jaskiewicz
Walter Johnson
Ernie Kamber
Mrs. William Kloepfer
Mrs. Jean Koser
Dave Krogseng
Miss Jeanette Lerner
Mr. and Mrs. Edward A. McCabe
George D. McCarthy
Jerome McGranaghan
Mr. and Mrs. Beverly Mason, Jr.
Don Melbe
Mrs. Fred C. Milner
Mr. and Mrs. Walter Mitchell
Phil Morrow
Miss Theresa Neises
Mrs. Theodore Newman, Jr.
Capt. Michael O'Connell, Jr.
Mrs. Loren Olson

CONTINUED

Young America's Salute

Youth played a major role in the inaugural festivities. Young America's Inaugural Salute included a ball held at the Washington Hilton Hotel on the Saturday before the inauguration and a brunch the next day at the same hotel to honor the younger appointees of the incoming administration. The pretty twins at the left were among the ball guests, as were Julie and David Eisenhower, above, and Tricia Nixon, shown at the right in happy conversation with friends, including her escort, Douglas Rogers (center).

The All-American Gala, held at the District of Columbia Armory two days before the inauguration, was a standing-room-only event. At left, Mr. Agnew addresses the audience. Below, the theme of the upcoming inaugural was emblazoned on the backdrop. Many performers took part; a few of them are pictured here, including the Drum and Bugle Corps of the famed United States Marine Band.

The All-American Gala

An intense James Brown belts it out.   *A long-time favorite, Connie Francis.*   *Tony Bennett, easy-does-it balladeer.*

Mama Lou Parks and the Parks Girls, a group that performs with Lionel Hampton's band.

Rufus Peckham
John Peterson
Mrs. Charles Potter
Pierre Purvis
Mrs. Jackson A. Ransohoff
Mrs. Charles R. Richey
Miss Nancy Sargent
Mrs. Francis B. Saul
Miss Catharine D. Scott
Mrs. John P. Sears
Mrs. Richard M. Simpson
J. Lewis Smith III
Mrs. Jack Marshall Stark
George E. Steele
Charles Stiles
Mrs. Richard H. Strodel
Mrs. Nancy Swinburne
Mrs. Edward T. Tait
William Taylor
Mrs. Ida Smith Taylor
Mrs. Gail Thiele
Peter Velde
Jack Venable
Merlin Veren
Mrs. Langhorne Washburne
Mr. and Mrs. H. Douglas Weaver
Miss Cynthia Weller
Miss Sharon Welles
Tyson Whiteside
Mr. and Mrs. William S. Zerman
Mrs. Richard H. Zimmer

GRANDSTAND COMMITTEE

Lt. Col. Sam D. Starobin, Chairman
James A. Blaser, Vice Chairman
Thomas F. Airis, Vice Chairman
Walter Boyce, Jr., Executive Secretary

CONSTRUCTION SUBCOMMITTEE

A. James Clark, Chairman
John E. Copeland, Vice Chairman
Lt. Gen. William Cassidy
Donald Giampaoli
Nash Castro
Walter Truland
Norman L. Biggs

DESIGN AND DECORATION SUBCOMMITTEE

James P. Calmer, Chairman
James I. Porter, Vice Chairman
William Suite
Stanley A. McGaughan
Mortimer M. Marshall, Jr.
Edward B. Willard
Charles Atherton
Councilman Margaret A. Haywood
Steve Kloss

INSPECTION SUBCOMMITTEE

John A. Israelson, Chairman
James D. Doughtie, Vice Chairman
Carl Hansen
Julian Dugas
John P. Stoddard
Theodore T. Smith
Charles E. Renner

INSURANCE SUBCOMMITTEE

Carl Anderson, Chairman
Francis C. Murphy, Vice Chairman
Kenneth Back
Edward D. Tracy
Clifford S. Chadderton

NEWS FACILITIES SUBCOMMITTEE

John Lynch, Chairman
Benjamin B. Lacy, Vice Chairman
William Monroe

SANITARY AND SNOW REMOVAL SUBCOMMITTEE

Burton F. Miller, Chairman
Norman Jackson, Vice Chairman
Col. Edwin G. Moran
William F. Roeder
R. Dana Wallace
B. J. O'Donnell
James C. Bailey

HOSPITALITY COMMITTEE

Harold D. Fangboner, Co-Chairman

Mrs. Harold D. Fangboner, Co-Chairman

VICE CHAIRMEN

Clarence G. Adamy
Mrs. Andrew C. Fretz
Henry J. Kaufman
Mrs. Corwin R. Lockwood
Harry Merrick, Sr.

HONORARY COMMITTEE MEMBERS

Howard C. Adams
Charles K. Brown, Jr.
Gen. and Mrs. Donald S. Campbell
C. Thomas Clagett, Jr.
Blake Clark
Karl W. Corby
Thurman Dodson
Mrs. Charles E. Eckles
Mr. and Mrs. Edward L. Feggans
Rogers M. Fred, Sr.
Harvey B. Gram, Jr.
Col. Albert P. Hinckley
Miss Marthajane Kennedy
Mrs. Mayme Mehlinger
J. Carter Perkins
Mrs. Paulus P. Powell
Mr. and Mrs. Donald Richardson
Mr. and Mrs. Nelson C. Roots
Col. and Mrs. Alexander G. Stone
Mrs. Ida Smith Taylor

COORDINATORS

Mrs. Harry G. Bandemer
Mrs. Paul G. Brauer
Mrs. Stuart M. Charlesworth
Mrs. William B. Clatanoff
Mrs. Winston Crickenberger
Mrs. L. Lawrence deNicola
Mrs. Fred Epson
Mrs. Rennie Kelly
Mrs. Edward Kenehan
Mrs. Barrington Parker
Mrs. Arch Scurlock
Mrs. James P. Sullivan
Mrs. Edward T. Tait
Mrs. J. Laning Taylor
Mrs. Bernard Zeavine
Mrs. Herbert L. Zincke

CAPTAINS

Mrs. Frank B. Alderson, Jr.
Mrs. Charles G. Aschmann, Jr.
Mrs. Edwin Atwood
Miss Alice Banks
Mrs. John Barrow
Mrs. Glenn P. Bieging
Mrs. Lavell M. Bigelow
Mrs. Samuel D. Botts
Mrs. Sanford L. Bransom
Mrs. Rita Brown
Mrs. Frank Carroll
Mrs. Michael P. Cericola
Mrs. James Chapman
Mrs. Charles Clements
Mrs. James M. Copeland
Mrs. Eldon W. Cox
Mrs. Howard R. Davis
Mrs. Mary C. dePalo
Mrs. Julian Dugas
Mrs. J. Glen Dyer
Franklin S. Everts
Mrs. David Fuss
Mrs. Charles J. Genovese
Mrs. Cecile Grant
Mrs. Helen E. Gray
Mrs. Alan Harquail, Jr.
Mrs. John C. Harris
Mrs. Fred W. Herbst, Jr.
Miss Lucile Hertz
Mrs. Welford H. Jackson
Miss Theresa Karger
Mrs. Scott Kirkley
Mrs. Reed Larson
Mrs. Nan Margolis
Mrs. John Martin
Mrs. Frederick Marvil
William Matthews
Mrs. Magnien McArdle
Mrs. W. H. McKinney
Mrs. James B. Morrison, Jr.
Mrs. Charles P. Murray
Mrs. Mary H. Myers
Mrs. Dale Ness
Mrs. Theodore Newman
Mrs. Robert Noble

Mrs. Ardle O'Hanlon
Mrs. Orin D. Parker
Mrs. Eileen Petrillo
Mrs. George C. Pierce
Mrs. Donald Pitts
Mrs. Barbara Porter
Mrs. Jack Rogers
Mrs. William T. Rooker, Jr.
William H. Sargent
Mrs. Robert Schwarzmann
Mr. and Mrs. John Sheffey
Mrs. James Shepard
Mrs. Marie A. Snellings
Mrs. Richard L. Spears
Mrs. Joseph H. Sullivan
Mrs. Julia B. Terry
Mrs. William S. Thompson
Mrs. Marvin Toombs
Mrs. George E. Travers
Mrs. Otis E. Troupe
Mrs. Merlyn Veren
Miss Lisa Waldeck
Miss Lynda Webster
Mrs. George Cabell Williams
Mrs. Dean E. Willmann
Mrs. Richard Wood

VOLUNTEER STAFF

Mrs. Elizabeth Boylan
Mrs. Leonidas T. Delyannis
Mrs. John A. Hetzer
Mrs. Lawrence Jacobsen
Carroll E. Joynes
Mrs. James B. Kelly
Mrs. Rosalie D. Miller

HOUSING COMMITTEE

Donald S. Bittinger, Chairman
Shirley K. Landon, Executive Secretary
John C. Pyles, Jr., Vice Chairman
John A. Norlander, Vice Chairman
Clarence A. Arata, Vice Chairman
Stewart Bainum
Twila T. Bennett
John Buck
John F. Craver
Austin Kenny
John La Spada
William McConnell
Charles H. Simmons

INAUGURAL BALL COMMITTEE

Mark Evans, Chairman
Mrs. Leslie Arends, Co-Chairman
Henry Berliner, Jr., Assistant to Chairman
Donald K. Duvall, Executive Director
Winston Childs, General Counsel
Chester R. Sellner, Comptroller
Lawrence Brailsford, Associate Director
Dr. John L. Clay, Associate Director
John E. Schrote, Special Assistant
Lynn N. Peterson, Jr., Special Assistant
Lt. Col. Earl C. McSwain, Staff Assistant

SPECIAL ADVISORS ON ARRANGEMENTS

Mrs. Gilbert Hahn, Jr.
Christian E. Stengel

ADMINISTRATIVE AND SECRETARIAL STAFF

Mrs. Christine Heina
Mrs. Ruth Kilroy
Mrs. Helen Lange
Miss Kathleen LeVan
Miss Melinda May
Mrs. Deborah Mueller
Mrs. Lorraine Otranto
Miss Leslie Schaberg
Miss Joyce Streeter

INVITATIONS AND TICKETS SUBCOMMITTEE

Mrs. Wayne W. Parrish, Honorary Chairman
Mr. and Mrs. John E. Packard III, Co-Chairmen
Mrs. June W. Taylor, Special Assistant
Mrs. James W. Bernhard
John Bowles
Mrs. George W. Dick
Mrs. Marcella Miller duPont
George M. Ferris, Jr.
Mr. and Mrs. Webb C. Hayes III
Mrs. Julian Kay
William R. Merriam
Robert Nesnick

Mrs. Dara Nordlinger
Richard Sebastian
Mrs. Ruth Sharon
Mr. and Mrs. Richard T. West

BOX SUBCOMMITTEE

John W. Kluge, Honorary Chairman
Robert M. Clark, Chairman
Alan J. Moore, Vice Chairman
Burr Allegaert, Coordinator
Mrs. Clyde McCoy, Secretary
A. C. Oliphant
Hillman Zahn

DECORATIONS SUBCOMMITTEE

John H. Walker, Honorary Chairman
Fred B. Zoll, Jr., Chairman
Mrs. Charles Weber, Special Advisor
Mrs. Neil Carothers, Special Advisor
Mr. and Mrs. Ralph E. Becker
Mrs. Ella M. Gothard Bransom
Mrs. Morris Cafritz
Mr. and Mrs. Charles Gray Cooper
Mr. and Mrs. Elliott DeGraff
Mr. and Mrs. Ben C. Evans, Jr.
Mr. and Mrs. Peter Frelinghuysen
Mr. and Mrs. George Goodrich
Lady Norma B. Lewis
Mrs. Corwin Lockwood
Hon. and Mrs. William Minshall
Lt. Gen. and Mrs. Elwood Quesada
Miss Catherine D. Scott
Mr. and Mrs. Edward Virgin
Mr. and Mrs. John W. West

FAVORS AND MEDALS SUBCOMMITTEE

Mrs. George E. C. Hayes, Honorary Chairman
Mrs. George Burnham IV, Chairman
George Burnham IV, Vice Chairman
Mrs. A. Guillermo Arrango
Mrs. F. V. duPont
Mrs. George A. Garrett
Mr. and Mrs. Richard B. Griffin, Jr.

MUSIC AND ENTERTAINMENT SUBCOMMITTEE

Mrs. Rose Saul Zalles, Honorary Chairman
Robert Cross, Chairman
Murrel J. Ades
Mrs. Catherine J. Brown
Mr. and Mrs. Curtis Munson
H. Gabriel Murphy

PROTOCOL SUBCOMMITTEE

Julian Dugas, Honorary Chairman
Mr. and Mrs. Scott Heuer, Jr., Co-Chairmen
Mr. and Mrs. Charles T. Matheson, Co-Chairmen
Clement E. Conger, Special Advisor
Norman Armour
Carroll Morgan
Hon. Jefferson Patterson
Carleton D. Smith
Douglas R. Smith
Gerard C. Smith
Miss Carol S. Wray

SAFETY AND SECURITY SUBCOMMITTEE

Milton W. King, Honorary Chairman
Howard V. Covell, Chairman
William E. Neumeyer
John W. Sweeterman
George D. Webster

TRANSPORTATION SUBCOMMITTEE

Gilbert C. Greenway, Honorary Chairman
Jack E. Brown, Chairman
Adm. Parke H. Brady, USN (Ret.)
Buckley M. Byers
Col. and Mrs. J. Hunter Drum
Maj. Gen. Thomas C. Musgrave, Jr.
Phillip H. Watts

PARKING SUBCOMMITTEE

James H. Lemon, Honorary Chairman
Kingdon Gould, Jr., Chairman
W. Bruce Alexander, Staff
Robert Amory, Jr.
Donald S. Farver

PUBLICITY SUBCOMMITTEE

Mrs. Leonard Silverstein, Chairman

Robert Siegrist, Co-Chairman
Joseph M. Clarke
Miss Jean M. Kossavides
Mrs. McCullough Darlington

SITE ARRANGEMENTS SUBCOMMITTEE

Kenneth E. Bemis, General Site Coordinator
Mrs. Mary-Stuart Diefenbach, Special Assistant
Mr. and Mrs. George Bunker
Alexander B. Hagner
Martin R. West, Jr.

MAYFLOWER HOTEL

Mrs. Berkeley Burrell, Honorary Chairman
Mr. and Mrs. Timothy D. McEnroe, Coordinators
Mr. and Mrs. Patrick O'Donnell,
    Hospitality Advisors

SHERATON PARK HOTEL

Dr. Henry Lucas, Jr., Honorary Chairman
Mr. and Mrs. Edgar Gillenwaters, Coordinators
Mr. and Mrs. Raymond Walsh, Hospitality Advisors

SHOREHAM HOTEL

Hon. Donald Lukens, M.C., Honorary Chairman
Robert H. Campbell, Honorary Co-Chairman
Mr. and Mrs. A. J. Somerville, Jr., Coordinators
Mr. and Mrs. Mandell J. Ourisman,
    Hospitality Advisors

SMITHSONIAN INSTITUTION

Charles R. Richey, Honorary Chairman
Mrs. Ralph Becker, Honorary Co-Chairman
Barrington Parker, Honorary Co-Chairman
Mrs. John M. King, Honorary Co-Chairman
Mr. and Mrs. Gant Redmon, Coordinators
Mrs. Elaine Lady, Hospitality Advisor
Mrs. Jean Koser, Hospitality Advisor

STATLER HILTON HOTEL

Mr. and Mrs. Gilbert Grosvenor, Honorary Chairmen
Norman O. Jarvis, Honorary Co-Chairman
Mr. and Mrs. Karl W. Flocks, Coordinators
Mr. and Mrs. Ray Brophy, Hospitality Advisors

WASHINGTON HILTON HOTEL

William S. Thompson, Honorary Chairman
Mrs. Perkins McGuire, Honorary Vice Chairman
Mr. and Mrs. Richard Ward, Coordinators
Mr. and Mrs. John W. Snow, Hospitality Advisors
Mrs. J. Clifford Folger, Senior Hostess

SPECIAL GROUP COORDINATION

Renah Camalier, Chairman
Jack Mills, Vice Chairman and Congress Liaison
George R. Rodericks, Civil Defense
William B. Burnham, Jr., Presidential and
    Vice Presidential Liaison
Bernard S. Van Rensselaer, Senior Citizens
Ben Cotton, Young Citizens
John Nidecker, Inaugural Committee Liaison

INSURANCE COMMITTEE

G. Dewey Arnold, Chairman
Norment Custis, Vice Chairman
Lawrence C. Dalley, Jr.
Lisle T. Lipscomb
Robert H. McDermott
William G. Russell
Victor O. Schinnerer
J. D. Marsh
Ralph W. Lee III
William Perkins, Jr.
Jerome J. Harris

LAW AND LEGISLATION COMMITTEE

F. Elwood Davis, Chairman
George E. C. Hayes, Vice Chairman
Harold A. Kertz, Vice Chairman
Arthur M. Becker
Melvin M. Burton, Jr.
Thomas J. Dougherty
Richard W. Galiher
Thomas S. Jackson
Roland F. Kirks
Richard G. Kleindienst
Richard K. Lyon
John Y. Merrell

Thomas F. Moyer
Godfrey L. Munter
Theodore R. Newman
Bernard I. Nordlinger
Kenneth W. Parkinson
Charles E. Pledger, Jr.
John E. Powell
John T. Sapienza
Jesse R. Smith
John Lewis Smith III
John L. Sullivan
Glen A. Wilkinson
Wesley Williams

MEDAL COMMITTEE

Dr. Melvin M. Payne, Chairman
Ralph E. Becker, Vice Chairman
D. Randall Buckingham, Vice Chairman
Milton L. Elsberg, Vice Chairman
Hon. Mark O. Hatfield, Vice Chairman
Mark B. Sandground, Vice Chairman
Hon. Fred Schwengel, Vice Chairman
John Walker, Vice Chairman
Eileen Young
William Flynn
Caroline Woyevodsky
Pauline Burns
J. Stephen Ramsburgh
S. Meyer Barnett
Thomas M. Beers
Windsor P. Booth
Mrs. Elvira Clain-Stefanelli
Ben W. Cotten
Willard R. Dick
Robert C. Doyle
Paul Ertzinger
Leonard J. Grant
Edward J. LeFevre
William T. Louth
Richard E. Pearson
Gerald Scher
Edwin W. Snider
Fred B. Zoll, Jr.

MEDICAL COMMITTEE

Milton C. Cobey, M.D., Chairman
William H. Cooper, M.D., Co-Chairman
Henry S. Robinson, Jr., M.D., Co-Chairman
Dorothy H. Fletcher, Secretary

VICE CHAIRMEN

Francis H. Cobb
Frederick Heath, M.D.
Col. John C. Ladd
Rear Adm. Rufus J. Pearson, Jr.
Col. Otis Snyder
Col. Walter Tkach
Maj. Warren Davis, WRAC
David H. Bachhuber, M.D.
Wyrth P. Baker, M.D.
William M. Ballinger, M.D.
Robert Beck
Samuel M. Becker, M.D.
Col. Latimer H. Booth
Roy N. Brown, M.D.
William Bucher
Vice Adm. George C. Burkley, M.D.
Robert V. Choisser, M.D.
Frances Chucker, M.D.
Charles H. Clark, M.D.
Fredericka R. Cobey, M.D.
Robert J. Coffey, M.D.
Darrell C. Crain, M.D.
Brig. Gen. Henry C. Dorris
George Dudas, M.D.
Charles H. Epps, M.D.
William H. Esch, M.D.
Carnot Evans, Jr., M.D.
Col. Raymond Fernandez
Paul V. Freese
Maj. William R. Gardner
Herbert M. Giffin, M.D.
J. Robert Gladden, M.D.
Michael Halberstan, M.D.
Wilbur Jackson, M.D.
J. Parran Jarboe, M.D.
Jack Kleh
Col. Walter A. Kostecki
John W. Latimer, Jr., M.D.
Allen Lee, M.D.
Daniel A. Leonard
William Loften, Jr., M.D.
Tanner B. McMahon, M.D.
Edward C. Mazique, M.D.
H. S. Meek
Col. Perry B. Miller
Raymond Osbourn, M.D.

CONTINUED

The Governors' Reception

The Governors' Reception on January 19 drew a crush of people to the Sheraton Park Hotel. The guests worked their way between rows of state stalls in which the various governors and their wives waited to shake hands and sign autographs. One non-governor assigned a place in the reception was Mrs. Alice Roosevelt Longworth, Theodore Roosevelt's daughter, who has added sparkle and wry humor to Washington social life since before the turn of the century. Among the other greeters were, at left, Governor and Mrs. Daniel J. Evans of Washington; at bottom left, Governor Walter Peterson, Jr., of New Hampshire, talking to Mrs. Dorothy L. Kelly and Comdr. Garland Sponburgh; below, Governor and Mrs. Claude R. Kirk of Florida.

Above, Governor and Mrs. John A. Love of Colorado.

At right, Governor Raymond P. Shafer of Pennsylvania and Governor Richard J. Hughes of New Jersey chat with Governor and Mrs. Nelson A. Rockefeller of New York.

George Pierce
Robert S. Poole, M.D.
Herbert P. Ramsy, M.D.
Lawrence A. Rapee
John W. Ridenour, M.D.
Robert Rizi
Robert C. Rush
Joseph T. Roberts
William F. Roeder
Capt. Jerome J. Schnapp
Cdr. Francis E. Senn, Jr.
Maj. Harold H. Shively
Francis L. Smith, M.D.
Robert Smith, M.D.
Robert Smith, D.D.S.
Theodore T. Smith
Col. Maxwell W. Steel, Jr.
Alfred J. Suraci, M.D.
Richard T. Sullivan, M.D.
Cdr. Norman E. Taylor
Arvel Tharp, M.D.
Capt. Max G. Walter
George D. Weems, M.D.
Don S. Wenger, M.D.
Edward R. Wernitznig, M.D.
Joseph Rogers Young, M.D.
Capt. Robert H. Zeff
Miss Joan Boyek, R.N.
Mrs. Pearl Craig, R.N.
Miss Lee Gillis, R.N.
Miss Sarah Glindmeyer, R.N.
Mrs. Doris Hutchinson, R.N.
Miss Patricia Johnson, R.N.
Miss Mary Keyes, R.N.
Miss Ann Rapee, R.N.
Miss Kate Thomas, R.N.
Miss Mary Ann Wall, R.N.
Mrs. Rhoda Yoder, R.N.

PARADE COMMITTEE

Edward R. Carr, Sr., Inaugural Parade Chairman
Robert A. Collier, Float Committee Chairman
Clarence Arata, Parade Vice Chairman
Thomas Sheridan, Parade Vice Chairman
Lt. Col. Paul Miller, USA (Ret.), Chief of Ceremonies
Capt. P. J. Murphy, Military Liaison Officer

ASSISTANTS TO THE CHAIRMAN

Bill Bartlett
Michael Woodson
Miss Sally Inge
John Taylor
Bill Belford
Doug Van Der Linden
Robert Byrne
Mrs. Linda Carter

MILITARY ASSISTANTS

Lt. Col. E. D. Bennet
Lt. Col. William H. Disher
Lt. Cdr. John R. Lawson
1st Lt. J. R. Proudfit

HONORARY MEMBERS

Franklin P. DeMarco, Jr.
Mark Sullivan, Jr.
Lt. Gen. Clovis Byers
Lloyd B. Wilson, Jr.
Curtis S. Steuart
Harrison Somerville, Sr.
Foster Shannon
Charles E. Phillips
C. William Martin, Jr.
E. Taylor Chewning, Jr.
Basil Winstead
Lawrence I. Wood
Winston W. Marsh
Hurlow M. Ralph
Daniel Clarke

VOLUNTEERS

Miss Marie Warme
Mrs. Alfred Mittendorf

PUBLICITY COMMITTEE

Fred Morrison, Chairman
Paul Theis, Vice Chairman
Richard Hollander
John H. Kauffmann
Ray F. Mack
John W. Thompson
Miss Vivian Huhn
Robert Bruce Amdur
Mrs. Thomas C. Skinker

Clyde Thomas Linsley
Miss Mary Margaret Anderson
Alvin Silverman
Gustav Jacob Miller
Felix Cotten
Mirek J. Dabrowski
Edward Samuel Segal
James Cameron Blakely
Joseph M. Sherman
William S. Fleishell
Mrs. Said Khan
Mrs. Thornton W. Owen
Lawrence E. Jones

VOLUNTEERS

John B. McDonald
Mrs. John W. Myers
Miss Lisa Baker
Keith Belch
Mr. and Mrs. Jack Downs
Jackson Eaton
Glen E. Loflin
Marshall Seibel
Mrs. Alvin Silverman
Miss Susan Silverman

PUBLIC SAFETY COMMITTEE

Chief John B. Layton, Chairman
Assistant Chief Jerry V. Wilson, Vice Chairman
Deputy Chief James M. Powell
Director James J. Rowley
Chief Grant Wright
Chief Hugh A. Groves
Thomas F. Airis
Thomas W. Bishton
Assistant Chief John S. Hughes
William D. Heath
Capt. Claude W. Dove, Aide to the Vice Chairman
Capt. Theodore R. Zanders, Secretary

METROPOLITAN POLICE
DEPARTMENT SUBCOMMITTEE

Chief John B. Layton, Chairman
Assistant Chief Jerry V. Wilson, Vice Chairman
Assistant Chief Lawrence A. Hartnett
Assistant Chief Charles L. Wright
Assistant Chief John S. Hughes
Deputy Chief George R. Donahue
Deputy Chief Raymond S. Pyles
Deputy Chief Joseph V. Osterman
Deputy Chief Charles Burns

TRAFFIC SUBCOMMITTEE

Thomas F. Airis, Chairman
R. Dana Wallace
John E. Hartley
Charles R. Sullivan
Seward Cross

CABLES AND BARRICADES
SUBCOMMITTEE

Thomas W. Bishton, Chairman
Paul V. Freese

PASSES AND PERMITS SUBCOMMITTEE

Assistant Chief John S. Hughes, Chairman
Inspector Aubrey C. Woodard
Lt. James L. Faircloth

MOTOR VEHICLES SUBCOMMITTEE

William D. Heath, Chairman
Herman S. Cole

RADIO AND TV BROADCAST
PROMOTION

BROADCAST PROMOTION UNIT

Robert C. Diefenbach, Consultant
Keith R. Belch
John P. Cosgrove
Ronald A. Davidson
Mrs. George W. Dick
Mrs. Janet Green
Miss Dorothy Herbert
Miss Judy Martin
Miss Rebecca Overton

BROADCASTERS GROUP

Harry H. Averell
Floyde E. Beaston
Alfred Beckman

Robert M. Bennett
John F. Burgreen
Warren Carmichael
John Corporon
William Dalton
Daniel Diener
Pierre D. Eaton
Neal J. Edwards
Connie B. Gay
Joseph Goodfellow
Milton Grant
Howard B. Hayes
Robert Howard
J. Alvin Jeweler
Harry A. Karr
Peter B. Kenney
Theodore I. Koop
William J. McCarter
Stephen J. McCormick
Theodore McDowell
E. Carlton Myers, Jr.
Lamar A. Newcomb
Andrew M. Ockershausen
Peter V. O'Reilly
John H. Pace
Bill Sanders

RELIGIOUS OBSERVANCE
COMMITTEE

Judge Boyd Leedom, Chairman
Rabbi A. Nathan Abramowitz, Co-Chairman
Rt. Rev. William F. Creighton, Co-Chairman
Rabbi Harry J. Kaufman, Co-Chairman
Rev. Graydon E. McClellan, Co-Chairman
His Eminence Patrick Cardinal O'Boyle,
    Co-Chairman
Pres. Milan D. Smith, Co-Chairman
Rev. Charles L. Warren, Co-Chairman
Randolph E. Stime, Executive Director
Wesley G. Pippert, Public Information
Laura H. Wilcox, Secretary
Rev. Andrew J. Allen
Rev. Seth R. Brooks
Rev. Dr. Clarence Cranford
Rev. Dr. Edward L. R. Elson
Rev. Canon C. Leslie Glenn
Rev. S. Everette Guiles
Rev. John C. Harper
Rev. John L. S. Holloman
Rev. James B. Joy
Rev. Demetrios G. Kalaris
Bishop John Wesley Lord
Rev. Jerry A. Moore, Jr.
Very Rev. Francis B. Sayre, Jr.
Rev. Dr. James M. Singer
Rev. E. C. Smith
Most Rev. John S. Spence
Rev. Clyde W. Taylor
Dr. D. Elton Trueblood
Rev. Carlton W. Veazey
Rev. Eugene O. Wright

SPECIAL GROUPS
PARTICIPATION COMMITTEE

Rev. Martin J. McManus, Co-Chairman
Earl Kennedy, Co-Chairman
Celso Moreno, Co-Chairman
Robert L. Bennett, Co-Chairman
Clarence L. Townes, Jr., Executive Director
Edwin T. Sexton, Jr., Assistant Executive Director
Shirley Browne, Executive Secretary
Ronald Davidson, Staff Assistant
Dr. John Armstead
Charles B. Fisher
George Lewis
Leon Perry

AMERICAN INDIAN SUBCOMMITTEE

John L. Belindo
Forrest J. Gerard
Dr. Ely Hurwitz
Solomon McCombs
Dwayne LeBeau
Dr. Browning Pipestem
Mrs. Betty Steinmetz
Dr. Paschal Sherman
Dr. James Wilson
Mrs. Helen M. Scheirbeck, Coordinator
Julie Thompson, Secretary
Edna Boggs, Secretary

LATIN AMERICAN SUBCOMMITTEE

Dezi Arnaz, Chairman
Rafael E. Vega, Jr.
Hilary Sandoval
Albert Fuentes, Jr.

Dr. Ray Pizano
George Sandoval
James Fresques
Hon. Junio Lopez
Hon. Leo Dow
Salvador A. Romero

SPECIAL SERVICES COMMITTEE

William Armstrong, Chairman
J. Howard Kautz, Executive Vice Chairman
Stan Barry, Vice Chairman
C. Lynn Lady, Secretary
Betty Jewell Rios, Secretary

BADGES AND INSIGNIA

Alden G. Barber, Vice Chairman
Mrs. La Verne A. Moore
Mrs. Ann Rawlinson

COMMUNICATIONS AND ELECTRONICS

Maj. P. Dudley Fischer, Vice Chairman
Albert L. Armstrong
Mrs. Mary R. Piranian
Lawrence O. Price
John L. Wolfgang

CARILLONS

Rev. Edgar D. Romig, Vice Chairman
Garnell S. Copeland, Carillonneur
Mrs. Doris J. Dillinger

LIAISON

John C. Hirschi, Director of Control Center
Herbert S. Rosenberg
Robert D. Cunningham, Inaugural Ball
Nathan K. Fields, Inaugural Ball
Harold P. Ganss, Sr., Inaugural Concert
Harold J. Ganss, Jr.
Richard Larimer, Governors Reception
Lt. Gen. Albert Watson II, Guard of Honor
Robert H. McAleese, Guard of Honor
A. Smith Bowman, Distinguished Ladies Reception
Richard D. Martinides, Inaugural Gala

PARADE

Milton A. Barlow
Anthony E. Ciuca
Dale O. Frazier
Bill Harnesberry
Carlos Vargas
Delmer H. Wilson

GRANDSTAND OPERATIONS

Fred D. Maise, Vice Chairman
Donald S. Clymans
George Dexter
Carl E. Hildebrand
Andrew J. Murphy
Kenneth B. Spear

GRANDSTAND TICKETS

John F. Morrissey, Vice Chairman
Mrs. Thea L. Boone, Vice Chairman
Leo Morrissey
Mrs. Sophia O'Neill
Mrs. Genevieve Emmons
Stella Masemer
Fran Davis
Roger Appold

TICKET COLLECTION

Roy C. Swab, Vice Chairman
Simon Lowry
William Powell

USHERS AND SUPERVISORS

L. Ray Torpy, Vice Chairman
William D. Hagins
Donald B. Pyle
Mark Schmutzler
Tom E. Snavely

PUBLIC RELATIONS

Rebel L. Robertson, Vice Chairman
Edward Belason
William Craft
Morris V. Rosenbloom
William T. Vincent
Mrs. Gertrude P. Worthington

MAINTENANCE

James Goedon, Vice Chairman
Erik Nystrom
William Scott Root
James O. Williams

COMMISSARY

William D. Beebe, Vice Chairman
Robert Beck
Mary A. Buckler
Michael Johnson
Benjamin Klopp
Mrs. Maude Katzenbach

STATE SOCIETIES COMMITTEE

Lewis E. Berry, Chairman
Clifford R. Paulson, Vice Chairman
Barbara L. Bullard, Secretary
Sally Court, Secretary

TRANSPORTATION COMMITTEE

William Calomiris, Chairman
Moe Lerner, Executive Vice Chairman
Ralph Becker, Vice Chairman
Godfrey Butler, Vice Chairman
Leonard B. Doggett, Jr., Vice Chairman
Robert V. Donahoe, Vice Chairman
Joseph V. Osterman, Vice Chairman
Osby L. Weir, Vice Chairman
Robert W. Bannon, Executive Director
William Creekmore, Special Assistant
Mrs. Alexander Laszlo, Administrative Assistant
Wayne Irwin, Coordinator
Lawrence Jones, Coordinator
Cdr. Carl Courtright, Coordinator
Charles M. Wicks, Coordinator
Frank E. Glaine, Coordinator
William S. Cohen, Coordinator
William Scullion, Jr., Special Assistant
M. L. Colton, Dispatcher
Mrs. Robert K. Boyer, Secretary
F. W. Ackerman
Floyd Akers
Thomas Appleby
George Avery
Ernest L. Barcella
Virgil E. Boyd
Jack Brown
Roy Chapin
Edward M. Clark
Jack H. Cohen
Edward N. Cole
Teunis F. Collier
Joseph Danzansky
S. A. DeStefano
William Donlin, Jr.
Hon. William O. Doub
James H. Drum
Henry Ford II
Thomas M. Goodfellow
John E. Hartley
George T. Higgins
Claude A. Jessup
Stanfield B. Johnson
George F. Kachlein
Irving Kator
S. E. Knudsen
Richard Kronheim
C. M. Lo
William V. Lundburg
Rodney W. Markley, Jr.
Claude Mathis
Beverly C. May
Brooks McCormick
William R. Merriam
Woodrow W. Miller
Nicholas Oganovic
Jack Pry
Anthony Richitt
James M. Roche
John Forney Rudy
John Ryan
Lt. C. W. Sine
Fred W. Smith
Lt. James F. Spicer
Thomas K. Taylor
Angelo C. Tompros
Lynn A. Townsend
Gerald H. Trautman
Hon. John A. Volpe

UNITED CITIZENS COMMITTEE

Charles S. Rhyne, Honorary Chairman
Hon. Louise Gore, Honorary Co-Chairman
John W. Warner, Honorary Co-Chairman

Michael Doud Gill, Chairman
William H. G. FitzGerald, Executive Vice Chairman
Biehl P. Clarke, Administrative Vice Chairman
E. Gay Fletcher, Executive Director
Mrs. John S. D. Eisenhower,
  Honorary Vice Chairman
Gen. Emmett O'Donnell, Jr.,
  Honorary Vice Chairman
Richard M. Scaife, Honorary Vice Chairman
Carlton F. Andrus, Vice Chairman
Dr. Joseph Aschheim, Vice Chairman
Norman R. Beebe, Vice Chairman
Mrs. William F. Burdick, Vice Chairman
Roger A. Clark, Vice Chairman
Val Choslowsky, Vice Chairman
Hon. Joseph S. Farland, Vice Chairman
Mrs. Dale Grubb, Vice Chairman
James Ackers, Vice Chairman
Philip A. Guarino, Vice Chairman
Andrew Jank, Vice Chairman
Richard Kiefer, Vice Chairman
Victor Kamber, Vice Chairman
R. Cy Laughter, Vice Chairman
John O. Padrick, Vice Chairman
Thomas A. Pappas, Vice Chairman
Ellis J. Parker, Vice Chairman
Lloyd X. Smith, Vice Chairman
Marshall Soghoian, Vice Chairman
Craig Truax, Vice Chairman
Bernard Van Rensselaer, Vice Chairman
Richard E. Wiley, Vice Chairman
Richard Gill, Jr., Comptroller
Mrs. Lydia Aguilar
Lyndon Allin
Ray Anselmo
William C. Archer
Warren Atkinson
Robert B. Baker
Michael C. Ballantine
John F. Beamer, Jr.
George T. Bell
James L. Berger
Jack Bierach
Sam Botts, Jr.
Walker B. Buel
Ralph Cake
Henry E. Catto, Jr.
Mrs. Robert S. Cooper
Richard Danner
James M. Day
Earl Dickson
Joseph Dobal
Dr. Lev E. Dobriansky
Mr. and Mrs. Dwight David Eisenhower II
Tony Faillace
Reese Fullerton
Theodore Gaffney
Robert Garfield
Frank P. Genduso
Don Goldie
Louis Graff
Karl C. Grannan
Mrs. Joseph H. Hariston
Ilmar Heinaru
Lewis H. Helm
Sally Hendon
Harry A. Hewett
Talley R. Holmes, Jr.
C. Dirck Keyser
Charles A. Lawson
Mrs. Stuart J. Long
Harry Lucas
Melquides Magabilem
Mr. and Mrs. William C. Mason
Vern I. McCarthy
Ed McMahon
Miss Robin McManus
Judie Mertz
Mr. and Mrs. George Gordon Moore
Joe Morgen
Robert R. Mullen
Mr. and Mrs. Herbert J. Muriel III
Gerald Schuyler Page, Jr.
Duane Patterson
Albert Pechan
Charles Peckham
John W. Pettit
Mrs. Eileen Pickering
Mrs. Richard Janik
Leland McLean
Hugh O'Brien
Larry R. Pilot
Harry E. Polk, Sr.
Joseph Pollard
Fred Radewagen
Mrs. Ogden Reid
Daphne Rimmer
Jan Rus
Tom Seagears
Mrs. Jane Schumann

CONTINUED

In the receiving line at the Vice President-elect's Reception are members of the Agnew family: Mr. Agnew, his wife, daughters Susan and Kimberly, and son Randy's wife, Ann. The reception was held inauguration eve, January 19, at the Smithsonian Institution. For the first time in history, the event was treated as an official part of the inaugural festivities, reflecting the incoming President's determination to bolster the prestige of the second office.

The Vice President's Reception

At the left, Mrs. Eisenhower looks at the gown that she wore to a state dinner for England's Queen Elizabeth and Prince Philip. With her is S. Dillon Ripley II, president of the Smithsonian and chairman of the Inaugural Concert. Below, Secretary of Defense-designate Melvin R. Laird and his wife hurry in to the reception.

Below left, Kimberly Agnew greets Mrs. Eisenhower. Right, among the arriving guests (between two staff members) are Postmaster General-designate and Mrs. Winton M. Blount, and House minority leader Gerald R. Ford and his wife.

Hal Short
Mrs. Willard D. Smith
Richard J. Smithson
Carlyle V. Stewart, Jr.
John T. Stewart, Jr.
Harry F. Stimpson, Jr.
Marsha Summerlin
Mrs. Don M. Sweet
Corcoran Thom, Jr.
William E. Timmons
Walter Troutman
George Wein
James G. Wilkinson
Miss Allaire Williams
W. Walter Williams
John F. Wolfe
Hon. Edward J. Derwinski
Matt Kane
Joseph J. Micciche
Louis Maniatis
Ralph Marcarelli
Ralph Perk
A. Edward Sandula
Mrs. Patricia Kinney
Gerald Pyszka
John D. Marsh
Bob Coe
Basil R. Littin
Miss Jackie Stein
Martin Nemetz
James H. Van Alen
Tony Michaels
Wylie Whisonant

VETERANS' PARTICIPATION COMMITTEE

Edward F. McGinnis, Chairman
Waldron E. Leonard, Co-Chairman
A. Leo Anderson
J. Raymond Bell
John P. Bowler
Col. John T. Carlton
Benjamin H. Chasin
Francis H. Cobb
Erle Cocke, Jr.
Robert A. Collier
Eli Cooper
James V. Day
James G. Dunton
Fred During
James C. Evans
LeGrand Fitchthorn
William B. Gardiner
Marshall C. Gardner
Richard P. Golick
Sidney S. Green
Paul H. Griffith
Ralph E. Hall
William F. Hauck
Mary C. Hanley
Charles Heck
Cooper Holt
John J. Keller
Robert S. Kelly
Frank R. Kossa
Robert N. Larson
Michael Locker
James E. McElroy
John T. Martin, Jr.
James J. Murphy
Luther Skaggs, Jr.
Eleanor Smith
Samuel Stavisky
Harris Stone
Francis W. Stover
Frederick T. Unger
James E. Van Zandt
James C. Watkins
H. Douglas Weaver
Fred S. Witte
Otto Zambreny
Victor V. Miller

ADVISORY SUBCOMMITTEE

Joe Foss
Harry W. Colmery
Timothy J. Murphy
James F. O'Neil
Frank Schwengel
Arthur G. Trudeau
Mrs. Waldron E. Leonard, Secretary
Dorothy Jordan, Secretary

VICE PRESIDENT'S RECEPTION

Hon. Louise Gore, Co-Chairman

Hon. Charles S. Bresler, Co-Chairman
Douglas G. Mode, Executive Director
Mrs. Paul F. Grooms, Assistant to the Chairmen
Robert E. Redding, Treasurer
Mrs. Wilmer A. Ullmann, Assistant Treasurer
Mrs. Joseph A. Mattingly, Administrative Assistant
Mrs. Robert E. Frese, Executive Secretary
Mrs. James Sullivan, Secretary
Miss Julie Bennett, Receptionist

HONORARY VICE CHAIRMEN

Hon. William P. Rogers
Hon. David M. Kennedy
Hon. Melvin R. Laird
Hon. John N. Mitchell
Hon. Vinton M. Blount
Hon. Walter J. Hickel
Hon. Clifford M. Hardin
Hon. Maurice H. Stans
Hon. George P. Shultz
Hon. Robert H. Finch
Hon. George W. Romney
Hon. John A. Volpe
Hon. Robert P. Mayo
Hon. Everett M. Dirksen
Hon. Gerald B. Ford
Hon. Marvin Mandel
Hon. Theodore R. McKeldin
Hon. Millard B. Tawes
Hon. Charles McC. Mathias
Hon. Joseph D. Tydings
Hon. Rogers C. B. Morton
Hon. Edward A. Garmatz
Hon. George H. Fallon
Hon. Lawrence J. Hogan
Hon. J. Glenn Beall, Jr.
Hon. Samuel N. Friedel
Hon. Gilbert Gude
Hon. C. Stanley Blair
Hon. Frances B. Burch
Hon. Louis L. Goldstein

INVITATIONS SUBCOMMITTEE

Don R. Kendall, Co-Chairman
Mrs. Corwin R. Lockwood, Jr., Co-Chairman
Mrs. Clinton Sisson

TICKETS SUBCOMMITTEE

Donald G. Roberts, Co-Chairman
Mrs. Donald G. Roberts, Co-Chairman

MUSIC SUBCOMMITTEE

Mrs. Lowell Mason, Co-Chairman
Mrs. Robert E. Maersh, Co-Chairman

PROTOCOL SUBCOMMITTEE

Jay Parker, Co-Chairman
Hon. Elaine Lady, Co-Chairman
John Peter Irelan
Robert J. Miller

SECURITY SUBCOMMITTEE

Lee Lauren, Co-Chairman
Leonard Viner, Co-Chairman
Hollis W. Bowers
John Chase
Bartley A. Costello
Allen H. Crawford, Jr.
Herbert J. Cronin
Fred E. Davis
Kevin F. Flanagan
Leo Milwit
Phillip Sachs
Leonard P. Steuart II
Pearson Sunderland, Jr.

DECORATIONS SUBCOMMITTEE

Paul Raymond, Co-Chairman
Mrs. Arthur M. Love, Jr., Co-Chairman

MEDICAL LIAISON SUBCOMMITTEE

Dr. William Walsh
Dr. Herbert L. Tanenbaum

PROGRAM SUBCOMMITTEE

Mrs. Istvan Botond, Co-Chairman
Mrs. Grant Johnston, Co-Chairman
Mrs. Paul Hatch
Miss Irenee Juno

LIAISON SUBCOMMITTEE

Robert Bird, Co-Chairman
Col. Peter Tanous, Co-Chairman
Alan Ehrlich
Mrs. W. T. Leith
J. D. Neal

SMITHSONIAN OPERATION SUBCOMMITTEE

William C. Birely, Co-Chairman
Charles R. Richey, Co-Chairman

TRANSPORTATION AND PARKING SUBCOMMITTEE

Kingdon Gould, Co-Chairman
J. Paull Marshall, Co-Chairman

SPECIAL PROJECTS SUBCOMMITTEE

George W. White, Jr., Chairman

PUBLICITY SUBCOMMITTEE

Mrs. Peter B. Rosenwald III, Co-Chairman
Mrs. Thomas C. Skinker, Co-Chairman
Jack Surrick
Herbert L. Thompson

DISTINGUISHED GUESTS SUBCOMMITTEE

Mrs. Don R. Kendall, Chairman
Mrs. Edward Clarke
Mrs. Stanley Cook
Mrs. Daniel Cronin
Mrs. J. Hunter Drum
Mrs. John Stuart McInerney
Mrs. Harvey Meyerhoff
Mrs. Roy St. Lewis
Mrs. Richard M. Simpson

FLOOR COMMITTEE

Hon. Thomas M. Anderson, Jr., Co-Chairman
Hon. James R. Miller, Jr., Co-Chairman
John P. Bankson, Jr.
Louis R. Baumgaertner
Allen M. Bost
Thomas Y. Canby, Jr.
James Chillis
Herbert Coles
Gus Constantine
Edward G. Courey
Col. Carlos D. Cutler
Hon. Frank A. DeCosta
Howard Denis
Hon. William B. Doub
Julian Dugas
John D. Duke
Stanley Eckles
John C. Eisele
Donald G. Ellerton
James F. Fanseen
David Fentress
Paul L. Fowler
Robert L. Ginesi
Harold Gould
W. Lee Hammer
Michael D. Hathaway
Paul M. Hawkins
George Heinze III
John L. Hill
M. Dale Hill
Joseph Hillings
Gerard F. Holcomb
Paul B. Kern, Jr.
N. Richard Kimmel
Raymond G. LaPlaca
Jerome K. Lyle, Jr.
Joseph C. McLaughlin
Charles S. Mack
Louis Maniatis
J. F. Morris
Joseph E. O'Brien, Jr.
Drapher Pagan
John Paterakis
Leon N. Perry
Robert H. Plante
Byron E. Pope
Edward A. Potts
Joseph N. R. Poulin
William J. Rowan III
Don H. Rowe
Leonard Silverstein
Robert V. Smith
Alvie Spencer
Douglas R. Stephenson
James Threatle

Hon. Sterling Tucker
Sylvester Vaughns
Frank Wade
Robert D. Vallick
Val Washington
George F. Weast, Jr.
Curtis White
David B. Wolfe
Herbert G. A. Woolley
Robert A. Yost

HOSTESSES

Mrs. Edward F. Kenehan, Co-Chairman
Mrs. A. Burks Summers, Co-Chairman
Mrs. John Aitken
Mrs. S. A. Alexander
Mrs. Edwin Atwood
Mrs. Alvin Aubinoe
Miss Cornelia Ann Babington
Mrs. Robert Beall
Mrs. James W. Bernhard
Miss Barbara Bird
Mrs. Charles Bloedorn
Mrs. Isaac Bortman
Mrs. Ella Mae Bransom
Mrs. Earle Palmer Brown
Mrs. Leland S. Brown
Mrs. Mary S. Budd
Mrs. James S. Bugg
Mrs. William R. Bush
Mrs. Peter Cameron
Mrs. Dorothy Captain
Mrs. Donald Carmichael
Mrs. David Chalmers
Mrs. John P. Cissell
Mrs. William D. Clarke
Miss Betsy Conway
Mrs. James Cooper
Mrs. Frederick J. Cullen
Mrs. Gordon Dean
Mrs. Leonidas Delyannis
Miss Kathryn E. Diggs
Mrs. Charles T. Donnelly
Miss Betty Lou Dotson
Mrs. James Burden
Miss Minny Eckles
Mrs. John F. Ellis
Mrs. Ralph Endicott
Mrs. Lee Edwards
Mrs. John Floyd
Mrs. Andrew Fretz
Mrs. David Fuss
Mrs. Mary Garner
Mrs. Paul Gomory
Mrs. H. Grady Gore, Jr.
Mrs. Kenneth Gould
Mrs. Ralph E. Grimm
Mrs. Robert A. Grosselfinger
Mrs. Harry V. Hayden
Mrs. George Hermanson
Mrs. Gordon Hirtle
Mrs. James Hogan
Mrs. John Hoover
Mrs. Henry Hornthal
Mrs. Donald S. Ihrig
Mrs. John M. Irvin
Miss Kathryn Jenkins
Miss Martha Johns
Mrs. J. Raymond Keany
Mrs. Mark A. Keefe
Mrs. Clarence Kefauver
Mrs. Earl Kennedy
Mrs. Wilkins Kennedy
Mrs. N. E. Kirby
Mrs. Hal Lackey
Mrs. C. W. Lamont
Miss Stephanie Lauren
Mrs. James E. Leasure
Mrs. Thomas E. Leitch
Mrs. Theodore R. Lettis
Mrs. John R. Lewis
Mrs. Warren Low
Mrs. Mary McHenry
Mrs. Joseph C. McLaughlin
Miss Ann McKay
Mrs. Yvonne McVay
Mrs. George W. Malone
Mrs. John S. Martin
Mrs. Gregg Martineau
Mrs. Leonard M. Mason
Mrs. W. Beverly Mason, Jr.
Mrs. Edward M. Meyer
Mrs. Berwyn Miller
Mrs. James R. Miller, Jr.
Miss Marilyn Mode
Mrs. Robert S. Mode
Mrs. Louis Montague
Mrs. Nicholas T. Nonnemacher
Mrs. Henry T. Offterdinger

Mrs. Thomas R. Ottenstein
Mrs. Virginia Page
Mrs. Ellis J. Parker III
Miss Gertrude Parker
Mrs. Charles Richey
Mrs. Frank Russell
Mrs. Joseph S. Ryan
Miss Carlota Savarese
Mrs. A. Thomas Schade
Mrs. Arthur Schroeder
Mrs. Arch Scurlock
Mrs. Claude J. Shiflet, Jr.
Mrs. Leonard Silverstein
Mrs. William P. Sims
Mrs. George Smith
Mrs. Richard Snyder
Mrs. Carlin Spragins
Mrs. Norvell Stearn
Mrs. Earl B. Steele
Mrs. Rex Sturm
Mrs. Berkley Sweet
Mrs. Evellyn Taggart
Mrs. Garvin E. Tankersley, Jr.
Mrs. Julia B. Terry
Mrs. Marion Thomas
Mrs. William Twaddell
Mrs. Mundy van der Meersch
Miss Cynthia Weller
Mrs. G. Louis Weller, Jr.
Mrs. L. H. Welsh
Mrs. John G. Werneke
Mrs. Horace K. Whalen
Mrs. Douglas Whitlock II
Mrs. John Whitney
Mrs. Robert J. Wright
Mrs. S. Harry Wright
Mrs. Herbert L. Zincke

VOLUNTEER PARTICIPATION

J. R. Pat Gorman, Chairman
Mrs. Dorothy Burkhardt, Vice Chairman
Mrs. Ab Hermann, Vice Chairman
Mrs. Richard M. Simpson, Vice Chairman
Miss Ann Babington
Mrs. Robert Beck
Hon. William H. Brett
Mrs. Vincent Callahan, Jr.
Mrs. Thomas H. Creighton, Jr.
Mrs. W. M. Crickenberger
Mrs. David Fuss
Mrs. James B. Gilbert
Mrs. J. R. Pat Gorman
Mrs. Robert B. Iglauer
Hon. Donald M. Jackson
Miss Therese Karger
Mrs. Gilbert Keech
Miss Catherine M. Krieg
Mrs. Henry O. Lampe
Mrs. Anthony Lausi
Mrs. Crawford Maddox
Mrs. Charles C. Majer
Mrs. Carole Martineau
Mrs. Robert Mullen
Mrs. Herbert J. Mulqueen
Mrs. Dale R. Porter
Mrs. Edward A. Potts
J. Field Reichardt
Charles R. Richey
Dr. James Shepperd
Walter Shipe
Mrs. Wayne H. Smithey
Mrs. Eileen Stathes
Miss Ella C. Werner
Mrs. Horace K. Whalen
Felton W. Wright

STAFF

Paul G. Lydens, Executive Director
Miss Kathy O'Melia, Executive Secretary
Mrs. Bernice Robertson, Secretary
Mrs. William Roy Harris, Jr.
Cpl. Milton A. Bailey, USMC

VOLUNTEERS

Miss Chris Adams
Mrs. Olga Bacher
John Ballard
Mrs. Edward Ballow
Miss Inez Barnard
Mrs. Joan Baylor
Miss Martha Beach
Mrs. Robert John Beaton
Mrs. Patricia Benson
Mrs. James W. Bernhard
Miss Chris Berquist
Mrs. Gloria Bothwell
Miss Kathleen Bovello

Mrs. Dot Brafford
Mrs. Mary Lou Brennan
Mrs. Harvey Bresler
Mrs. Ruth Brett
Mrs. Judith L. Brown
Miss Patricia Burrell
Mrs. C. W. Cardin
Mrs. Vera Casto
Norma Chiriboga
Mrs. Sarah Clark
Mrs. John Conley
Miss Erma L. Corry
Mrs. Anna Cote
Mrs. Peggy Crawford
Mrs. Georgianna Delyannis
Mrs. Walter Demer
Mrs. Robert W. Eby
Mrs. William E. Farren
Miss Patricia Flasher
Mrs. Evelyn Flory
Mrs. Rosemary Foreman
Mrs. Thelma Fruitman
Mrs. Helen Gehman
Mrs. Amy Gilreath
Mrs. Peggy Grady
Mrs. E. Charlton Graves II
Mrs. George Green
Mrs. Ann Haffner
Alexander Hamilton
Mrs. Phyllis Hanner
Mrs. N. Key Hart
Mrs. Charles Hartman
Mrs. Gretchen Heltzel
Mrs. Phillip Herrick
Mrs. Lucille Humphrey
Mrs. Walter Jacobs
Mrs. Anna E. Johnson
Mrs. Russell B. Johnson
Miss L. Alice Jones
Mrs. Ann B. King
Mrs. Dorna Kreitz
Mrs. Margaret Lancaster
Mrs. Cookie Laithe
Mrs. Francis Littlejohn
Miss Vera Lundquist
Mrs. Jeanne Lupton
Mrs. Ralph McCabe
Mrs. Shelly McCoy
Miss Mary Jane McKnight
Mrs. Louis Mehlinger
Mrs. Frederick Milner
Mrs. Erma Mittendorff
Mrs. Rosalind Modlin
Miss Lois Moore
Roger Moure
Mrs. Joan Munson
Mrs. Dorothy Neely
Miss Naomi Nelson
Robert J. Nesnick
Mrs. Dara Nordlinger
Mrs. Mary Partlett
Mrs. Vera Petschek
Mrs. Lucille Pinkerton
Mrs. Alice Reed
Mrs. Cecile Reeves
Mrs. Jane Ring
Salvador A. Romero
Miss Jane Schumann
Mrs. Ethel Sendlak
Miss Mary Sheehan
Mrs. Emilie B. Standish
Malvin Steinbach
Mrs. Elizabeth Stenger
Mrs. Doris Tartaglino
Mrs. Kenneth G. Tower
Mrs. Vera Vander Haeghe
Miss Mary Whitsall
Mrs. Betty Wynne

YOUNG REPUBLICANS

Jack McDonald, Co-Chairman
Dottee Fancher, Co-Chairman
Benjamin W. Cotten, Co-Chairman
Henry J. Hamilton, Vice Chairman
Kenneth C. Reitz, Vice Chairman
Theodore A. Cormaney, Executive Director
Barbara Bowie, Supervisor
Cathy Cargle, Publicity
Lyndon Allin, Special Youth Groups
Michael Hudson, Housing and Reception
Morton Blackwell, College Activities
Damion Dufour, Special Committee Luncheon
Dawn Young, Committee Secretary
Susan Tabb, College Committee Secretary
Margaret Gaynor, Secretary
Nora Vandersommen, Secretary
Winston Childs
J. Warner Hagan, Jr.
Arthur P. Hartel, Jr.

The Inaugural Concert

The sound of music enlivened much of the ceremony surrounding Mr. Nixon's swearing-in. The event traditionally devoted to music is the Inaugural Concert, and tickets to the 1969 edition at Constitution Hall were sold out forty-eight hours after they went on sale. All the pieces on the program were by American composers, and all the performers were Americans. Shown arriving at left are Mr. and Mrs. Nixon; below, Tricia and her escort, Larry Drown.

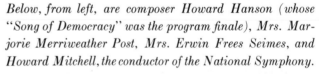

Above, the Nixons wave to the audience. Below is the Mormon Tabernacle Choir, which sang several pieces that evening, under the direction of Richard P. Condie, including "American Songs of Patriotism and Brotherhood."

Below, from left, are composer Howard Hanson (whose "Song of Democracy" was the program finale), Mrs. Marjorie Merriweather Post, Mrs. Erwin Frees Seimes, and Howard Mitchell, the conductor of the National Symphony.

The first Executive Mansion on Cherry Street, New York. It proved too small for the Washingtons' entertaining, and they soon moved to a larger house on lower Broadway.

170

The President's House

The White House is a venerable mansion now, and in remarkably good health for its almost 170 years of existence. In that time it has housed some notable tenants and witnessed unusual events. But probably nothing about the structure is as remarkable as that it has suffered so much adversity and neglect and yet still stands—for Presidents to live in and for citizens to admire.

George Washington was the only President who never lived in the White House. Two different houses served as Executive Mansions during the somewhat less than two years New York was the nation's capital; then in 1790 Philadelphia was made the capital and a mansion there on High Street became the President's House.

The building of a national capital on the Potomac began in 1792, and the Executive Mansion—designed by architect James Hoban—was near enough to completion for John and Abigail Adams to move in during November, 1800. Only about half a dozen rooms were even livable, the main staircase was not up, and the smell of damp plaster was everywhere. Abigail hung her washing in the unfinished East Room.

Long before the building was finished the British captured and burned Washington in August, 1814, during the War of 1812. A violent rainstorm came up in time to quench the flames and save the thick outer walls of the President's House. While the work of rebuilding was pushed, James and Dolley Madison found other quarters, nor did they ever return to the Executive Mansion, for it was not ready until the autumn of 1817, and by then James Monroe was President. The outside had been painted white to hide the scorch marks from the fire, and the residence became popularly known as the White House, although the term was being used as early as 1810 because of the light color of the stone exterior.

Even during the time of John Quincy Adams, who was inaugurated in 1825, the home of the nation's first citizen was so untidy that architect Charles Bulfinch observed that "no gentleman of moderate property would permit [it] as his own residence." But with the completion of the South Portico in 1824 and of the North Portico in 1829 the White House took on approximately its present appearance. Adams did much to landscape the grounds, and after him Andrew Jackson spent lavishly to furnish the Mansion.

Over succeeding years and with changing tenants, the house began to show signs of wear and tear. A complete examination made in 1871 found cracks in almost every ceiling (the ceiling in one room had fallen a year earlier), rotting timbers, and so many other evidences of deterioration that the report laconically noted, "It hardly seems possible to state anything in favor of the house as a residence." Two years later the Mansion was renovated in the height of the Victorian style, with overstuffed divans, heavy mirrors, deeply figured wallpapers, and great cut-glass chandeliers.

Only eight years later, in 1881, Chester Arthur redecorated the White House again. Arthur, very much of a dandy, called on the noted decorator Louis Comfort Tiffany, among whose innovations were much colored glass, including a huge stained-glass screen in the entrance hall, an abundance of heavy draperies, and tremendous quantities of gold paint. The Blue Room was changed to a robin's-egg shade.

The White House had suffered from serving as executive offices as well as residence. Mrs. Benjamin Harrison was the first to try to correct the situation. At her request an architect submitted plans about 1890. One proposal was to turn the White House into an executive office building and build a new President's House. Another plan would have added ungainly wings to the White House. Nothing came of the proposals, but a number of interior repairs were made and electricity was brought into the house.

New wings were proposed again in 1896 and in 1900, but the plans were condemned as monstrosities. Then in 1902, soon after Theodore Roosevelt became President, a West Wing for executive offices and a balancing East Wing were built, both connected to the White House by colonnades. The west colonnade incorporated a pavilion built for Jefferson in 1807; it was discovered when Victorian greenhouses were torn down to make way for the new wing. While the Roosevelts lived elsewhere for several months, the interior was also rebuilt. The former offices on the second floor became living quarters, and the Victorian exuberances, including President Arthur's Tiffany glass screen, were stripped away.

In 1927 the roof was so badly rotted that the Coolidges had to move out while roof, attic, and second-floor ceiling were removed and repaired. The former

The Octagon House (right) was home for James and Dolley Madison for a time after the British burned the White House. The old building still stands today, in good repair.

The etching of the White House from the south (below) was made in 1839 or 1840, and is romanticized and inaccurate. The rounded South Portico, for one thing, is depicted as solid, whereas it is actually made up of columns. Tiber Creek, in the foreground, was later filled in, and its bed today lies buried beneath Constitution Avenue.

Near the end of the last century, when the picture at the left was taken, the East Room was so cluttered that one almost needed a guide to get through it. The pillars and ceiling beams, huge gas chandeliers, and divans date from the Grant redecoration of 1873; the potted palms and other greenery were brought in from the White House conservatory largely by President McKinley.

Below, the White House stands completely gutted during the renovation of 1948–52. The framework of steel beams that will carry the weight of the interior has been put in place. Thus rebuilt and strengthened, the White House should endure for centuries.

The White House today is more than Executive Mansion; it has become a national shrine. No President now would dare to redecorate completely, as Chester Arthur did, and it is unlikely the Mansion will see any major changes.

attic was rebuilt with a higher roof to give a third floor with additional guest rooms.

During the generations and the administrations of many Presidents, the ancient timbers had been cut time after time to install plumbing and wiring. Walls had been pierced for doors. Important structural members had become weakened. In 1947 President Truman noticed that the floor of the Oval Room, his study, trembled under his footstep, and when a leg of his daughter's grand piano went through the floor, a committee of architects was called on to make a survey of the Mansion. They found portions of it in danger of collapse; in fact, the only thoroughly sound portions were the same outer walls that had survived the fire of 1814.

The Trumans moved out at once. A proposal to tear down the White House and build a new mansion, though the cheapest alternative, was discarded because of the sentiment and tradition around the old house. So all mantelpieces, woodwork, and the like were carefully marked, removed, and stored. The outside walls were underpinned by concrete piers, and the house was reduced to a mere shell, inside which was erected a steel

framework to carry the rebuilt interior. And finally the inside was reconstructed as before, with the original paneling and other woodwork replaced.

Mrs. John F. Kennedy took up the project of making the interior of the White House fittingly reflect the spirit of the American Presidency. In 1961 she formed a Fine Arts Committee to furnish the Mansion with noteworthy antiques and to redecorate the Mansion in something resembling its original classic style. As a result of the committee's work, the house has been redecorated, many old pieces recovered from storage, and treasures added through bequests.

Mrs. Nixon has said before and after the inaugural that she thought the Mansion beautiful and planned no changes. But even without redecorating, there is enough to do. The size of her new home is easier to grasp when it is considered that it has—to name a few items—132 rooms with 69 closets, 28 fireplaces, 30 crystal chandeliers, and 412 doors. To run her home, Mrs. Nixon will be helped by a household staff—chefs, maids, butlers, housekeepers, laundresses—of thirty-two men and women.

175

ACKNOWLEDGMENTS AND CREDITS

The Inaugural Story was created and produced by AMERICAN HERITAGE Magazine and the 1969 Inaugural Book and Program Committee.

The Staff for *The Inaugural Story:*

For the Book and Program Committee:

Editor: Robert Keith Gray
Associate Editor: F. C. Duke Zeller
Inaugural Research: Jane Johnson

For American Heritage:

Editor: Ralph K. Andrist
Associate Editor: Michael Harwood
Contributing Editor: David Jacobs
Art Director: Karen Bowen
Picture Research: Nancy Oakes
Text Research: Susan Baker
      Constance Corning
      Judith Pittenger

The 1969 Inaugural Book and Program Committee:

Hon. Robert Keith Gray, Chairman
F. C. Duke Zeller, Executive Vice Chairman
Robert R. Mullen, Vice Chairman
Herman F. Scheurer, Jr., Vice Chairman
Mrs. George Aiken
John Altorfer
Robert Amblad
Mrs. Howard Baker
Joseph H. Batchelder
Mrs. Edward Brooke
Mrs. George Bush
Mrs. Frank Cacciapaglia
Mrs. C. William Cardin
Hon. Harry Tyson Carter
Mrs. Claire Lee Chennault
Mrs. Donald Cook

G. Edward Cotter
Miss Catherine Croswell
Miss Ann Cuningham
Robin David
Miss Lynne Davis
Thomas Davis III
Mrs. Daniel Evans
Col. Charles William Freeman
Peter Ladd Gilsey
Mrs. Marie Gray
George Hall
Col. West A. Hamilton
Miss Peggy Harlow
Roy Harris
Mrs. Mark Hatfield
Henry W. Herzog

John W. Hill
Hon. Patrick J. Hillings
William D. Howard
Mrs. Roman Hruska
Miss Merlyn Hunger
Dewey Hutchins, Jr.
Mrs. Ronald Johnson
Mrs. Dorothy Kelly
Miss Karen Koon
Mrs. Chester Larson
Mrs. Robert McCormick
Mrs. Robert Michel
Mrs. Duane Miller
Mrs. Jack Miller
Miss Rosemary Murphy
Prof. Vera Newburn

Mrs. J. Allen Overton
Mrs. Charles Percy
Mrs. Ronald Reagan
Mrs. John Rhodes
Mrs. Doray Saddler
Peter M. Schluter
Mrs. William Scott
C. Carney Smith
Cmdr. Garland Sponburgh
Mrs. Anita Teshima
Mrs. W. Robert Thrall
William E. Towell
Mrs. John Tower
Mrs. Clyde Walters
James B. Walters
Bernard Waters

The Book and Program Committee wishes to express its appreciation to those who prepared stories on personalities and events of the 1969 inaugural: Mrs. Leslie Arends, Philip C. Brooks, Senator Everett McKinley Dirksen, the Honorable Robert Keith Gray, Dr. Frederick Brown Harris, Senator George Murphy, Gerry Van der Heuvel, and F. C. Duke Zeller.

The 1969 Inaugural Committee extends its thanks to the many companies who have made time, personnel, and services available, and especially its appreciation to Hill and Knowlton, International Public Relations Counsel.

Paintings of First Ladies' gowns, pp. 124–27, by Cal Sacks.

The Editors wish to thank Margaret Klapthor of the Smithsonian Institution for assistance in the preparation of the paintings of the First Ladies' gowns.

Photographs of 1969 inaugural events, where not otherwise credited, are by Capitol and Glogau, Washington.

The Editors also gratefully acknowledge permission to use material from the following books:

p. 136: *The Collected Works of Abraham Lincoln*, Vol. I. Copyright 1953 by The Abraham Lincoln Association. Reprinted by permission of Roy P. Basler.
pp. 137–38: *A Carnival of Buncombe*, edited by Malcolm Moos. Copyright © The Johns Hopkins Press 1956. Reprinted by permission of The Johns Hopkins Press.
p. 141: *The Letters of Theodore Roosevelt*, Vol. VI, edited by Elting E. Morison. Copyright 1952 by the President and Fellows of Harvard College. Reprinted by permission of Harvard University Press.
pp. 141–42: *A Puritan in Babylon*, by William Allen White. Copyright 1938 by The Macmillan Company. Reprinted by permission of William L. White.